Roots of Rastafari

D0972234

LOS GATOS H.S. LIBRARY

DISCARDED

From the
collection of
Mark Bradburn
English teacher
at L.S.N.S.
1962 - 1996

LOS GATOS H.S. LIBRARY

Roots of Rastafari

Virginia Lee Jacobs

DISCARDED

LOS GATOS H.S. LIBRARY

Slawson Communications, Inc.
3719 Sixth Avenue
San Diego, CA 92103-4316
(619) 291-9126

© 1985 Virginia Lee Jacobs

All rights reserved under International and Pan-American Copyright
Conventions, including the right to reproduce this book or portions thereof in
any form whatsoever, except for use by a reviewer in connection with a
review.

Excerpts from *Philosophies and Opinions of Marcus Garvey* by Amy Jacques-
Garvey. Copyright 1925 Amy Jacques-Garvey. Introduction Copyright 1968
Hollis R. Lynch. Reprinted with the permission of Atheneum Publishers, Inc.

Excerpts from *Days of Emperor and Clown* by James Dugan and Lawrence
Lafore. Copyright 1973 by Lawrence Lafore and Ruth Dugan as
Administratrix of the Estate of James Dugan. Reprinted with the permission
of Doubleday & Company, Inc.

Photographs courtesy of and with permission from Peter Simon, The Bettman
Archive, and Wide World Photos, Inc.

Ethiopian map courtesy of and with permission from Oxford University Press.

Library of Congress Cataloging-in-Publication Data
Jacob, Virginia Lee, 1951–
   Roots of Rastafari.

   "An Avant book."
   Bibliography: p.
   I. Ras Tafari movement — History. 2.Haile Selassie I, Emperor of
Ethiopia, 1891-1975. 3. Reggae music.
I. Title.
BL2532.R37J33 1985   299'.67   85-51342
ISBN 0-932238-25-4 (pbk.)

Published in 1985 by Avant Books
Slawson Communications, Inc.
3719 Sixth Avenue
San Diego, California 92103-4316
(Write for free catalog)

Cover and book design by Ed Roxburgh, San Diego, CA
Book Production by The Word Shop, San Diego, CA 92103-4316

Printing in the United States of America

10 9 8 7 6 5 4 3 2 1

299.6
J

BC #25979

Contents

The Roots of Ras Tafari is dedicated to
Josh Doolan
whose inspiration and insight brought this book
to life.

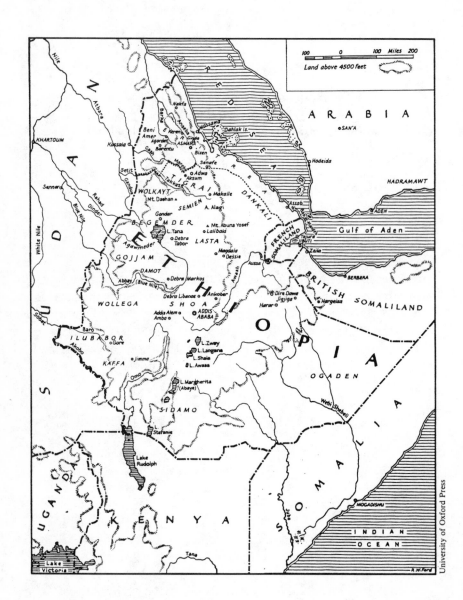

University of Oxford Press

Introduction

Ras Tafari is a name that is familiar to many, but understood by few. Most people do not know whether it refers to a man or a movement. The answer is both. At this time, the legendary tradition referred to as Rastafari has become an intricately interwoven fabric of fact and folklore. Perhaps the most revealing way to understand who or what Ras Tafari is, is to listen to the following words of a speech delivered by His Imperial Majesty Haile Selassie I at Stanford University in 1968:

> . . . that until the philosophy which holds one race superior and another inferior is finally and permanently discredited and abandoned; that until there are no longer first- and second-class citizens of any nation; that until the color of a man's skin is of no more significance than the color of his eyes; that until the basic human rights are guaranteed to all without regard to race; until that day, the dream of everlasting peace and world citizenship and the rule of international morality will remain but a fleeting illusion to be pursued but never attained. And until the ignoble but unhappy regimes that hold our brothers in Angola, in Mozambique, and in South Africa in subhuman bondage have been toppled and destroyed;

until bigotry and prejudice, and malicious and inhuman self-interest have been replaced by understanding and tolerance and goodwill; until all Africans stand and speak as free human beings, equal in the eyes of the Almighty; until that day, the African continent shall not know peace. We Africans will fight, if necessary, and we know that we shall win, as we are confident in the victory of good over evil.

To understand the Rastafarian movement is to understand the life of Haile Selassie, who is, in fact, the enigmatic Ras Tafari. Haile Selassie is regarded by the Rastafarians as a messianic figure. A direct descendant of the Judeo-Christian tradition, he claims his ancestry from King Solomon and the Queen of Sheba. At the same time, fundamental to his spiritual make-up is the Coptic Christian belief of *Monophysitism*, or the indwelling existence of Christ in each of us. In this sense, Ras Tafari *is* God, a proclamation often taken literally by many Rastafarians, who refer to their Messiah as *Jah*[1].

Haile Selassie may be recognized by conventional historians more as a political figure than as a spiritual one. Before he became emperor of Ethiopia, Ras Tafari struggled against the corruption, deceit, and excesses of political turmoil around him. Maintaining an admirably ethical posture, his ascent to power was a test of his moral as well as his political strength. Although Ras Tafari was groomed to inherit the throne from Menelik II at the age of 14 (circa 1906), destiny eluded the young man because of the mysterious death of his father, Ras Makonnen. After that tragedy, the young prince's life was in constant danger from others conspiring to gain royal power; but through perseverance and cunning, Ras Tafari was finally crowned Emperor Haile Selassie I in 1930.

His full title, His Imperial Majesty Haile Selassie I, King of Kings, Lord of Lords, Conquering Lion of the Tribe of Judah, Elect of God, Emperor of Ethiopia, bears an uncanny resemblance to the following quotation from the Book of Revelations in the New Testament:

And I saw in the right hand of him that sat on the throne a book written within and on the backside sealed with seven seals. And I saw a strong angel proclaiming with a loud voice, 'Who is worthy to open the book

neither to look thereon.' And I wept much, because no man was found worthy to open and read the book, neither to look thereon . . . And one of the elders saith unto me, 'Weep not: behold, the Lion of the tribe of Judah, the Root of David, hath prevailed to open the book, and to loose the seven seals thereof.'
Revelations 5:1-5

On this basis many Rastafarians regard Haile Selassie as an incarnation of God, as the black man's Messiah. When a delegation from Jamaica visited Ethiopia in 1961, the *abuna* (archbishop of the Ethiopian Orthodox Church) advised them against referring to His Majesty as the Messiah. He also said that such an implication was threatening to Haile Selassie's own beliefs as a devout Christian that Jesus Christ was the Messiah referred to in the Book of Revelations. However, orthodox Rastafarians interpret Haile Selassie's humility as further proof of his divinity.

In their insistence of Haile Selassie's divinity, zealous Rastafarians overlook the principle of monophysitism that was so much a part of the emperor's belief structure. Haile Selassie believed that the divine and human natures of Christ are one; and although he acknowledged the God within himself, he also acknowledged this as a reality available to all.

Ras Tafari has played a key role in the awakening of both spiritual and political consciousness among blacks. Interestingly, though, the Rastafarians owe as much to Marcus Garvey as they do to Haile Selassie for their creation as a group entity. In Jamaica during the 1920s, Marcus Garvey sought to uplift the oppressed and degraded lifestyle of blacks. Impoverished and miserable, black Jamaicans were forced into servitude by a minority population of British imperialists who ruled the islands. Garvey's philosophy was one of repatriation for all blacks whose ancestors were brought to the West as slaves. His slogan was "Back to Africa!" and his ultimate goal was to wrest colonial rule of Africa from the Europeans, reinstating blacks to their native lands. Garvey recognized Haile Selassie when he was crowned emperor as the man who would fulfill his hope for blacks around the world. So began the religion known as Rastafari, which refers to Ras Tafari and Jah, the Most High God, as one and the same.

Now fast becoming a spiritual path for many people — black and white — the religion, discipline, and music of Rastafari have spread into America, raising the movement beyond the status of a mere fad. The Rastafarians provide a new lifestyle for many, recognizing vegetarianism and fasting as a direct approach to God. Beyond the superficial appearance of the Rastafarians (their masses of uncut hair called *dreadlocks*, their reggae music, and the smoking of the herb *ganja*), there exists a tradition that emanates from an ancient source. The study of Haile Selassie provides a key to the unearthing of legend and history so profound that it demands definition of the Rastafarians in a universal light.

There is little point to attempting to establish whether Haile Selassie is or is not the Messiah. What is important is that his life has served as an example and an inspiration to the black nation which, until recently, had little knowledge of its great African heritage. Equally significant is recognition of his role as catalyst for the awakening of a sense of identity and history for the black people who have been scattered over the earth by the oppressions of slavery.

Haile Selassie died in 1975 as the Third World was beginning its emergence. In the twilight of his years, Haile Selassie fell from his glory as emperor and died in political disgrace. Although this book makes no real attempt to evaluate Haile Selassie as a political figure, it has become increasingly apparent that his performance as emperor presents a controversial issue that cannot be overlooked.

For many who choose to see him as such, Haile Selassie is a symbol of oppression. At the same time, for those who have a more spiritual interpretation of his life, he is a symbol of redemption. To the Rastafarians, the ancient Judeo-Christian tradition that Haile Selassie brought with him to the throne is a revelation, which may have some profound influence over the future history of Earth. The fact that the essence of Ras Tafari survives among the Rastafarians is in itself a type of resurrection and immortality.

It is a natural tendency to stand in judgement of Haile Selassie. However, the aim of this book is to present the historical facts about his life, spiced with the ancient legends of his ancestry, in order to convey the essence of who he was and what his movement is. The life of this most mysterious man has undeniably left its mark on the world, the historical truth of which has yet to be understood. To those who know him, the truth is clear, and for everyone else, a fascinating journey is about to unfold. Consider this book as a point of departure on an exciting voyage of discovery.

[1]Jah is probably a shortened version of the Jewish name for God, Yahweh or Jah-weh.

1

The Legend of Solomon and Sheba

Wwhat makes the story of Haile Selassie's coronation so glorious is the ancient tradition he brought with him to the throne. Ethiopian monarchs have taken pride in the fact that their dynastic line has been unbroken[1] since the great time of King Solomon of Israel and the Queen of Sheba. According to the *Kebra Negast* (one volume from the Ethiopian Royal Chronicles meaning "glory of the kings"), the Queen of Sheba was none other than Makeda, Queen of Ethiopia. Although there are other claims to the heritage of the Queen of Sheba (including Queen Belkis from Yemen in southwestern Arabia), considering all sources, it is most likely that the queen was indeed from Ethiopia. The Solomonic dynasty is regarded as the oldest surviving monarchy in the world, and with it came the worship of one true God and the principle of divine right. It is important to understand these ideas in order to understand the coronation and reign of Haile Selassie, what he meant to his people, and what he has come to mean to the Rastafari.

The legend of Solomon and Sheba is perhaps the most well-defined documented love story of all time, from the Bible and Shakespeare to the Koran and the Ethiopian Royal Chronicles. As the story goes, in about 1370 B.C., having replaced the last of the Arwé line[2] a ruler named Angabo began the dynasty to which

5

Makeda belonged. The way in which Angabo attained the throne is reminiscent of a fairy tale.

Apparently the country had been terrorized by an evil serpent Wainaba, a dragon monster. In their desperation, the rulers of the country promised the throne to whomever could kill the dragon and bring peace to the land. Angabo, a fearless man, stepped forward and agreed to undertake the monstrous task. Angabo had an ingenious plan: he fed the dragon a poisoned goat, and when the dragon fell asleep, he cut off its terrible head. The dynasty begun by Angabo ruled for 350 years, during which nearly twenty monarchs came to the throne, including Queen Makeda's grandfather, Za Sebado, her father, Za Sebado's Chief Minister, who married the king's daughter, and Makeda herself.

When Princess Makeda's brother, young prince Noural Rouz, was accidentally dropped into the fire as an infant, he left his sister as the only heir to the throne. Makeda reigned from about 1005 B.C. until about the year 955 B.C. She was apparently both beautiful and intelligent, and very rich.

A wealthy Ethiopian merchant, Tamrin, went to Jerusalem to trade with the Israelites. Among his customers was King Solomon, who was dazzled by the gold, sapphires, ivory, and ebony the merchant had brought. In turn, Tamrin was greatly impressed with Solomon's wisdom as a king and his knowledge of the one true God, Jehovah. He was also overwhelmed by the wealth and splendor of Solomon's palace, and the way he ruled his people with justice and kindness.

When Tamrin returned home, he told Makeda fantastic stories about this faraway land and the amazing man who was king. Queen Makeda was determined to make the journey to Jerusalem to see for herself whether these things were true. So, she journeyed to Jerusalem to find Solomon and to test him with difficult questions. She traveled with a great train of 800 camels bearing spices, gold, and precious jewels from her native land as gifts for the king. When she arrived, "she communed with him all that was in her heart" (I Kings 1:10). He in turn "gave unto the Queen of Sheba all her desire, whatsoever she asked" (I Kings 10:13). And the two fell deeply in love.

The queen was given accommodations in the royal apartments and was served food and drink from morning until night. During their hours of delightful conversation, the two turned to the subject of religion. When Solomon explained to her about the "one true God, the God of Israel,"³, she immediately abandoned the pagan worship of the sun, moon, trees, birds, spirits, and serpents, to embrace Jehovah (also known as Yahweh or Jah-weh), the God of Solomon.

After spending six wonderful months in the court of King Solomon in Jerusalem, Queen Makeda began to think about the duties that awaited her in Ethiopia. She knew, however reluctantly, that she had to return home to take care of her people. King Solomon was greatly distressed and attempted to keep her with him by proposing marriage. Although the temptation to stay and flourish under his guidance must have been difficult to refuse, Makeda was duty bound and determined to go home.

Solomon persuaded the queen to stay for a farewell banquet, at which time he served many rich and spicy dishes. He then entreated Makeda to spend the night in his chambers. Queen Makeda accepted only under the condition that Solomon would not try to seduce her. Solomon agreed to this, under his own condition that she not take anything that was his. Since she could think of nothing of his that she wanted, Makeda agreed to the condition. Having forgotten about the spicy meal that evening, Makeda awoke with a terrible thirst and drank deeply from a bowl of water that happened to be placed beside her. At that, the clever Solomon was released from his promise and took her to bed.

Several months later, Solomon realized that he could not hold his beloved against her will. It must have been difficult for him to let Makeda go, especially since she was expecting his child. Before her departure, Solomon gave the queen many presents to take with her, including a gold ring for their child should it prove to be a son. He blessed her, saying, "Go in peace and may the peace of God be with thee." At the outskirts of her kingdom, Makeda went into labor and delivered a baby boy named Ebna Hakim, which translates to English as son of the wise man.

As a gracious ruler, Queen Makeda brought prosperity to her kingdom. Ebna Hakim grew to be a fine young man who greatly resembled his illustrious father. Fulfilling a promise she had made to Solomon, Queen Makeda sent her son to visit his father in Jerusalem, bearing the gold ring as identification. The young man made the long journey with Makeda's aging chief minister, Tamrin. Solomon was overjoyed to discover that his son was endowed with many princely qualities, in contrast to his other son, Rheabom, who was considered a fool. As he had done with

Makeda, Solomon begged Ebna Hakim to stay to inherit his kingdom and rule the Israelites. But like his mother, the young man was anxious to return to his homeland and spread the knowledge of Jehovah among his people.

Solomon finally yielded to his son's resistance, willing to acknowledge an unseen destiny. To assist Ebna Hakim with his missionary intentions, Solomon arranged for the sons of his greatest counselors to accompany the youth on his return trip to Ethiopia. But the young Israelites felt as though they were being banished to a godforsaken part of the world and were reluctant to go into a pagan land. In light of this, Solomon arranged for a replica of the sacred Ark of the Covenant to be made — as a symbol of Jehovah's presence — for the travelers to take with them. The night before the caravan was to depart, the young Israelites mischievously substituted the replica for the real Ark. So, when they embarked upon their journey the following morning, the real Ark of the Covenant — the most sacred object in the Jewish faith — was in their possession.

The fate of the lost Ark, "too holy to be looked upon" by human eyes, has been one of the most wildly speculated topics of all time. It has been the subject of folklore and fantasy, both ancient and modern. According to legend from the *Kebra Negast*, the Ark currently rests somewhere in Ethiopia, probably buried deep in one of the rock-hewn monasteries in or near the ancient city of Axum, Queen Makeda's capital. When Solomon learned of its theft, he was devastated and sent his horsemen to catch the caravan and repossess the Ark. But the Ark's disappearance seemed to be God's will: "God himself confounded the pursuers by miraculously sweeping the caravan forward with such swiftness that it was never overtaken."

In his wisdom, Solomon realized that the vanished Ark was both an omen and an act of fate. He was powerless to alter the facts or recover the Ark. But Makeda and her son regarded these circumstances as part of their destiny, and the Israelites with their Ark and their new religion were most enthusiastically welcomed in Ethiopia. It is speculated that the descendants of these Jewish immigrants became known as the *Falashas*, black Jews of Ethiopia, who practice an extremely orthodox doctrine to this very day.

The seeds of the new faith were planted, and the religion of the one God flourished under protection of the Ethiopian monarchy. When Queen Makeda completed her benign rule, she was naturally succeeded by her capable son, who took the name Menelik I when he ascended the throne. He continued to use the city of Axum as his capital, and he based his government on the worship of Jah-weh and the law of Moses. The tradition of Jah-weh that was planted in Ethiopia 3,000 years ago survives today as Jah, the Rastafarians' name for God.

[1] The illegitimate Zagwé dynasty (the Agaus), which ruled in the twelfth century, abdicated the throne in order to perpetuate the *unbroken* lineage.

[2] The Arwé line most likely came from Egypt where the serpent was worshipped.

[3] William Leo Hansberry, *Pillars in Ethiopian History*. The remainder of the quotations in this chapter not referenced to a specific source are from this work.

2

Discovering Jah

Before the knowledge of Jah could come to the world, man needed to establish himself on the earth. According to recent anthropological research, what is now modern-day Ethiopia could well be the cradle of humanity. If, indeed, human life began in the Horn of Africa, it most likely took place in Ethiopia's great Rift Valley, a deep, wide swath of land that cuts through the mountainous terrain of the Ethiopian highlands and fans out into the coastal plains of the Red Sea. After millennia of seismic stress, this little-known geographic region has become the greatest anthropological hunting ground ever found.

THE EARLIEST DESCENDANTS

Recent finds by scientists at the University of California, Berkeley, offer proof that the origins of human life may be extended to four million years ago, one half million years earlier than the date previously established by discovery of what was believed to be the oldest human skeleton "Lucy." The discovery of both Lucy and her earlier descendant occurred in the area known as the Afar Triangle near the present-day borders of Tigre and Wollo in Ethiopia. Even more recently, in 1982, a fossil hunter from Kenya found in the Samburu Hills of his own country a fossilized jaw-

11

bone dating back an unbelievable eight million years. These latest remains help authenticate the theory that the first man walked the earth in East Africa.

These exciting discoveries predate even the most ancient lineage claims of East African cultures, including those of the ancient Egyptians. In fact, it is quite possible that the Egyptians, Ethiopians, and other East African cultures are descended from the sons of Noah, who intermarried with local inhabitants after the Great Flood of the scriptures. According to legend, Noah's Ark landed somewhere near the source of the Nile; not impossible if the floodwaters indeed covered the earth. Since the headwaters of the Nile are located in modern-day Ethiopia, it is likely that the descendants of Noah populated ancient Ethiopia, migrating east to the Red Sea and north along the Nile Valley into Egypt. Legend also reveals that the sons of Noah fathered the peoples of North Africa in the following way: Ham begat the Ethiopians; Shem begat the Canaanites; Mizraim begat the Egyptians; and Japheth begat the Libyans. Cush, one of the sons of Ham, established a kingdom between the second and fourth cataracts of the Nile, before this land became known as Egypt. In turn, Cush's son, Ethiops, settled the highland area which now bears his name, Ethiopia. The kingdom of Aksum (Axum) was founded by his son, Aksumawi, and thus began Ethiopian civilization.

When reviewing Ethiopia's long and distant past, it is useful to see how the ancient historians and geographers referred to the Ethiopians. The classic Greek writers classified all humans with brown or black skin under the general title of Ethiopian. This included people from Libya, Egypt, Cush (modern-day Sudan), Abyssinia (modern-day Ethiopia), and the rest of the natives of known Africa. Semitic authors differentiated correctly between the racial groups, referring to Ethiopians as non-blacks with dark skin, and labeling Negroid black Africans as *Cushites*, meaning those from the land of burnt faces.[1] Post-Christian writers, despite an awareness of the differentiation, referred to all northeastern Africans as Ethiopians, as did the Greeks, who thought of Ethiopians and Egyptians as one and the same people.

NUBIA: THE LAND OF GOLD

In the earliest times of recorded history, Egypt was the great civilization of Africa. To Egyptians, the land of Cush was a kind of no-man's land, beyond the fringes of the known world. Adventurous Egyptian traders would brave the journey up the Nile to get their legendary cargos of gold, ivory, and precious gems. Since gold came from Cush, the Egyptians began to refer to it as *Nubia*, which means the land of gold.

As the descendants of Noah migrated down the Nile Valley, with them went the vanishing knowledge of Jah-weh, the one true God. (Jah-weh, or Jehovah, the god of the ancient Israelites, is probably where the modern-day reference to Jah finds its origin.) Before long, worship of Noah's one true God was limited to a very few elite families. But through Aksumawi, the great-great-grandson of Noah, worship of Jah-weh survived in relative isolation, immune to the numerous other cults worshipping nature spirits and supernatural forces promoted by the surrounding native tribes. It was no small accomplishment that Aksumawi established a monotheistic culture in the ancient city we know as Axum.

It is also possible that the use of the Egyptian name *Amen* as a prenom for its kings, and later one of its primary gods, Amen Ra (also spelled Amon or Amun Re), was brought down the Nile into Egypt by the descendants of Cush, who retained a glimmer of the light of Jah-weh. Amen means the hidden or holy one; the name Amen Ra meant that the god dwelled within the king. Resemblance to the Judeo-Christian Amen, a blessing to the divine, is striking.

The earliest reference to Amen appears in the pyramid of King Unas. Amen is included among the primeval gods associated with *Nu*, the fathers and mothers from the *deep beyond* in the beginning. The deep beyond refers to heaven, or to the deeps of Africa, which to the Egyptians would be Nubia and beyond. Could it be that through the creation myths — which exclude any mention of the Great Flood — the Egyptians are remembering their ancestors, the sons of Noah, who came from the source of the Nile? The source of the Nile, which was the lifeblood of the Egyptians, was fearfully revered by them. One Ethiopian conqueror later achieved his victory over Egypt by threatening to divert the headwaters of the Nile and thus destroy Egypt.

Egypt split into Upper and Lower Egypt early in the late kingdom period, around 1075 B.C. One dynasty ruled at Tanis in Lower Egypt (where Aten was worshipped) and the other at Thebes in Upper Egypt (where Amen was worshipped). At this time, Nubia (or Cush) created a separate state upstream, with its vital trading port, Napata, as its capital. This was just prior to the time when the Queen of Sheba and her son, Menelik I, formally established the Axumite kingdom in Ethiopia.

CUSH RULES ANCIENT EGYPT

The kingdom of Cush reached its climax of power in the tenth century B.C., when it successfully captured Memphis (now Cairo) and Thebes and ruled Egypt for five generations of Cushite (Ethiopian) Kings. The story of Piankhi, the Cushite conqueror responsible for this, is related through Egyptian hieroglyphics found on a massive block of basalt in the temple of Amen at Jabar Barkal. One fascinating aspect of Piankhi's life was his devotion to Amen, since the Egyptian worship of Amen is similar to the Jewish worship of Jah-weh with its purification rites (including circumcision), prayers, holy of holies, and the divine succession of kings.

According to the hieroglyphs, when Piankhi conquered Thebes he went to give thanks for his victory at the temple of Amen, purifying himself with sprinklings of holy water and the burning of incense. With flowers and exotic perfumes in hand, he mounted the steps of the temple to look upon the face of his god, who was enclosed in a sort of tabernacle, behind bolted doors. Reminiscent of a scene from the Old Testament, Piankhi saw his god Amen Ra, face to face. The god, in permitting himself to be seen, acknowledged Piankhi as king of all Egypt and an instrument of his will. Under Piankhi's rule, the Cushite kingdom was extended from the Mediterranean to the highlands of Ethiopia.

After Piankhi's death, Shabaka, his nephew, conspired with King Hosea of Israel against the Assyrians (see II Kings 17:4). Because of this, the Assyrians invaded Egypt and forced the new ruler, Tirhakah (see Isaiah 37:9), to retreat deeper into Cush, moving their capital from Napata to the island kingdom of Meroe, three hundred and sixty miles farther up the Nile. Meroe became the permanent capital of Cush and had a ledgendary history all its own.

THE ISLAND KINGDOM OF MEROE

Meroe was important because it was another black civilization, independent of Egypt and Ethiopia. It was held in power by the Amen priesthood, which by this time had become corrupt and tyrannical. Meroe was a matriarchy ruled by the infamous Candace queens who were well known for their violent, warlike natures. According to one Greek historian, the people of Meroe believed in an immortal god who created the universe and a nameless mortal god whose nature was undefined. Although kings and royal personages were regarded as gods by the common man, those who worshipped trees, animals, and the elements of wind, sun, and rain believed that inhuman forms controlled the lives of most people.

The civilization of Meroe waxed and waned during the fourth century A.D. and eventually fell to the rising Axumite power to the east. The Axumites were also of Cushitic, or Hamite stock, since Ham was the father of Cush, who was the father of Ethiops and the grandfather of Aksum, who migrated up the Nile and founded the kingdom Axum after the Great Flood.

There was another group of immigrants to the Ethiopian highlands who arrived during the first millennium B.C. These were the Semites, also descended from Noah through one of his other sons, Shem. The Semites probably came from the region of Yemen, across the Red Sea in South Arabia. With them they brought the Sabaen language and culture, with the vowelless Himyaritic alphabet, as well as some knowledge of the Jewish faith.

ABYSSINIA

The name *Abyssinia* comes from the South Arabians who referred to the tribe living in Ethiopia as the *Habasha* and to their country as *Habash*. Since there was a negative immigrant connotation to this name, the Ethiopians disliked the name Abyssinia — which was usually used by Europeans — and chose to call themselves by their ancestor's name, Ethiops. Apparently the Hamito-Semitic tribes, or the Habashat, integrated with the Negroid races who inhabited the highland plateau of modern Ethiopia, and the two races intermingled to produce the handsome, intelligent, and graceful race of dark-skinned, fine-featured people we know as Ethiopians.

The Habashat immigrants from South Arabia found stark differences between their way of life and that of the native Hamites. The newcomers introduced metallurgy, to some extent, and brought knowledge of how to build houses and temples of stone. They also educated the natives, teaching them agricultural practices such as terracing the hillsides to fully utilize drainage and constructing earthen reservoirs to collect the valuable run-off waters from the hillsides, which had hitherto been allowed to dissipate among the desert sands.

The Semites who upgraded the standard of living in Ethiopia may be descended from several of the lost ten tribes of Israel, who supposedly reestablished themselves in the South Arabian peninsula. The Bible (see II Kings 15:29) tells how the king of Assyria defeated Israel and took all of the Israelites into bondage. Many of the tribes escaped and dispersed to points unknown. According to the ninth century historian, Eldad Ben Mahli Ha-Dani, the ten tribes settled in parts of South Arabia (referred to as Havilah), including Yemen, and ultimately even as far as Abyssinia.

THE FALASHAS

The story of Ethiopia's ancestral roots would not be complete without a close look at the Falashas, or black Jews of Ethiopia, the surviving evidence of the existence of an ancient Hebrew cult. The Falashas are a curiously devoted group of people who have clung stoically to their Semitic beliefs, even through the country's Christianization in the fourth century A.D. They have survived into the twentieth century, living in the mountainous Lake Tana region at the source of the Nile. *Falasha* is a Semitic word that means emigrant, and the Falashas usually refer to themselves as "beta Israel" or of the "House of Israel." Numbering between 15,000 and 60,000, the Falashas are fiercely independent and have fought numerous wars to preserve their freedom.

The Falashas' form of worship is based entirely on the Old Testament, especially the Pentateuch, which contains the five books of Mosaic Law. The Book of Jubilees, an apocryphal book of the Old Testament unknown to most Jews, is also very important to the Falashas. They, however, have no knowledge of the Mishnah or Talmud in their Torah and were not affected by any of the events that shaped the Jewish nation after the scattering of the ten tribes of Israel. For this reason, these black Jews do not carry the attitude of psychological persecution that has characterized the majority of Jewish peoples for the past two thousand years.

Like other Jews, the Falashas adhere to the Ten Commandments and the laws regarding cleanliness. Male children are circumcised on the eighth day after birth, a custom also observed by the Ethiopian Christians. Naturally, the Sabbath is a holy day (from sunset on Friday until sunset on Saturday) and is strictly observed. Fasting takes place not only on the Sabbath but on Mondays and Thursdays as well. Like orthodox Jews around the world, they do not eat pork or shellfish. They also observe the feast of the Passover, which became traditional for exiled Jews in Egypt just prior to Moses' deliverance, although they seem to know little about the later feasts. The Falashas tend to intermarry and keep to themselves; they do not want to be contaminated by outsiders.

Oddly, the Falashas do not speak Hebrew. Whereas the popular language of Ethiopia is *Amharic*, religious books are written in *Ge'ez*, or Ethiopic, an ancient language very much like Latin. Ge'ez may have found its roots in the Sabaen language and the Himyaritic alphabet imported from South Arabia by the Semite settlers. Ge'ez corresponds to the tribal dialects of Ethiopia (Amhara, Tigre, and Tigrinya) the way Latin relates to the romance languages (French, Italian, and Spanish).

The true origin of the Falashas is still a mystery. Even though it is likely that the worship of Jah-weh really took hold after the time of the Queen of Sheba and her son, Menelik I, circa 1000 B.C., Judaism as it is practiced among the Falashas in Ethiopia is probably older than that. The Falashas themselves claim descendancy from Abraham, Isaac, and Jacob. Because they possess so much knowledge of those ancient Jewish traditions that came into being *after* the time of the Jews' exile into Egypt, it is altogether possible that they are indeed one of the lost tribes of Israel.

THE NATURE WORSHIPPERS

Although Abyssinia was the home of an ancient Hebrew cult, monotheism at that time was the exception rather than the rule. Knowledge of Jah-weh existed in this area after the time of Noah, but Jah-weh soon became eclipsed by the popularity of the local deities and nature spirits worshiped by the native tribes. These nature worshippers, who comprised about ninety percent of the population, were hunters and gatherers concerned mainly with the realities of survival. Their worship of trees, snakes, birds, wild animals, stones, mountains, rivers, and the sun and moon was dictated by their dependence on these elements for their food. Desert dwellers existed on little more than snakes, lizards, and locusts. Rainforest people had a more imaginative selection of gods owing to their lush environment, as did the mountain people, with the wind and rain as the ruling elements of their day-to-day existence. Coastal dwellers, too, probably had rituals to guarantee the life-giving abundance of their main source of food, which was, of course, fish. In the face of such competition, it is no wonder that Jah-weh waned.

THE ADVENT OF JAH-WEH

It is well known that before the Queen of Sheba visited King Solomon in Jerusalem and converted to the one true God, Jehovah, she had worshipped the gods of her people. She probably bowed to the sun and moon like her ancestors of Yemen, as well as to a fertility goddess (who was also popular across the Red Sea). But after her visit to Jerusalem and conversion to Judaism, a religious reformation took place. Sheba's return to her homeland must have initially revived an interest in Jah-weh, but it was not until the birth of King Solomon and Sheba's son, Menelik I, that the worship of Jah-weh became the state religion. When he took his mother's place on the throne, Menelik I instituted a style of government based on the worship of Jah-weh and the Law of Moses. The importance of possessing the ancient Ark of the Covenant as a symbol of the light and will of God marked the establishment of a new era in the religious life of the people of Axum.

Menelik I was the first official king of Axum and united two conflicting lines of royal descent in the Ethiopian Royal Chronicles. Until now, the Ethiopian Chronicles have not been taken seriously by most historians because one king's list claimed descent from Noah through Ham and Cush, whereas the other king traced his lineage through one of Noah's other sons, Shem, and his descendant, Solomon. This does not present any real contradiction since the Hamite side reflects the maternal line of the Queen of Sheba, while the paternal Semitic line comes from Solomon. This union established the Ethiopian royal line from which Haile Selassie claims his descent.

During the fifth and sixth centuries B.C., the power of Axum once again declined, and it is likely that the worship of Jah-weh declined with it. As late as the fourth century B.C., superstition and witchcraft were reportedly prevalent among the Abyssinians once again. As Axum became an important trading city with Egypt and the rest of the Hellenized world, it became influenced by a mixture of Hebraic, Egyptian, and Greek cults, in addition to the local pagan deities of its ancestors.

THE ANCIENT CITY OF AXUM

Compared to the glorious accounts of Rome, not much is known about Axum. There is, however, an abundance of legend. Axum is situated at the head of a beautiful plain, almost between two hills. It is particularly lush, bearing seventy-two springs, and although the city itself rests on flat ground, it is surrounded by beautiful mountains. In ancient times, the city of Axum was an eight day journey from the seaport of Adulis. The Queen of Sheba is buried in Axum, and it has been a holy city since that time. There is also great speculation that the lost Ark of the Covenant, too holy to be looked upon, is carefully preserved somewhere in the city of Axum.

Axum's traders traveled by way of the Red Sea and the great caravan routes from Egypt, Mesopotamia, Constantinople, India, Ceylon, and Persia. Axum was actually the capital of an area called Tigre, and Tigre's ambassadors were held in great esteem by the ancient world. The chief exports of this area were gold, spices, precious stones, and rare incense.

The most impressive remains of the ancient city of Axum that can be seen today are the *stelae*. These stelae are obelisk-like monuments of granite rock, with an altar-like platform at their base. There is a good deal of mystery surrounding them because no one knows what they really are or why they were built. There are no inscriptions, only the recurring pagan symbol of a crescent-shaped moon cradling a sun disc. The stelae are about sixty feet high and are situated in a field not far from Axum. Perhaps they were memorials to the departed Axumite monarchs and were intended as dwellings for their spirits. The Ethiopians associate the stelae with the reign of the Queen of Sheba, which deepens their reverence for Axum as a holy city. Even in modern times, emperors have been crowned in Axum on an ancient stone seat in the shadow of the tallest stelae.

By the first century A.D., the Axumites had consolidated their power and won predominance over rival tribes of the area. By this time, their commanders-in-chief were using the title

Negusa Nagast, which means King of Kings. These words would later come to be synonymous with emperor, the same title used by Haile Selassie in the twentieth century. The political dominion of this new power stretched in the direction of Arabia from the east, to the northwest bordered by the Nile, where the kingdom of Meroe was in a state of decline. Axum stepped into the vacuum of power left by the increasingly ineffective Candace queens, destined to conquer Meroe by the fourth century A.D. This conquest expanded Axum's cultural horizons because it opened up trade with the Nile Valley and all of Hellenized Egypt.

By this time, the Greeks had been in power in Egypt for several centuries. Their emissaries had brought not only the Greek language to the Red Sea region, but they also had introduced the worship of the Greek gods, Zeus, Aries, and Poseidon. The Greek writer of the *Periplus* tells how all of the ivory from beyond the Nile came through Axum, and about the miserly (yet scholarly with respect to his knowledge of Greek literature) king named Zoscales who governed the area. In light of this history, it is likely that the Greeks had as much of an effect on the Axumite civilization as did the South Arabians or the Hebrews.

Between the first and fourth centuries A.D., the Axumites invaded and occupied South Arabia in the region of Yemen. During the end of the third century A.D., the Axumite ruler, King Aphilas, was in control of this region across the Red Sea, from which his ancestors had come. Aphilas, the great grandfather of Axum's greatest king, Ezana, minted and circulated coins stamped with the familiar pagan symbol of the crescent moon and solar disc. He was a strong king who had proven Axum's military might by establishing a materially secure and stable kingdom. Aphilas also laid the foundation for the advent of Christianity.

Several generations later, at the zenith of Axum's power, Aphilas's great grandson, Ezana, finally conquered Meroe and Christianized the kingdom of Axum. The seeds of Christianity were germinated. They flourished and became an island of faith amidst the sea of Islam, thus remaining uncorrupted by the politics of Roman Catholicism. It is this Ethiopian Christianity, in addition to Axum's distant Hebrew roots, that created the backbone of Haile Selassie's spiritual existence and has been transformed into the Rastafarian worship of Jah.

[1] Sir E.A. Wallis Budge, *History of Ethiopia*, pp. 164-165. The remainder of the quotations in this chapter not referenced to a specific source are from this work.

3

The Power of
the Trinity

Christianity first came to Ethiopia shortly after the time of Christ, which makes Ethiopia one of the oldest surviving Christian nations on earth. The story of the first Ethiopian Christian is well documented in Chapter 8 of the Acts of the Apostles in the New Testament.

THE FIRST CHRISTIANS

In the year 40 A.D., during the reign of an Ethiopian queen named Candace (Queen Garsemat Kandake VI),[1] who was a seeker of Jah-weh, the one true God, a most miraculous event took place. The apostle, Philip, had been told by an angel of the Lord to go during the noon hour across the road that led from Jerusalem through the Gaza desert. As he did this, the treasurer of Ethiopia, who is referred to in the Bible as a "eunuch of great authority," came down the road. His chariot approached, and Philip could hear him reading aloud from the book of the prophet Isaiah. Intrigued by what he heard, Philip drew closer. "Do you understand what this means?" he asked the stranger. "Of course not," replied the eunuch, "when I have no one to instruct me." The passage of scripture he had been reading aloud was this:

21

He was led as a sheep to the slaughter,
And as a lamb is silent before the shearers,
So he opened not his mouth.
In his humiliation,
Justice was denied him.
And who can express the wickedness
Of the people of his generation,
For his life is taken from the Earth.

As Philip began to speak, the eunuch begged him to come and sit with him in the chariot. "Was Isaiah talking about himself or someone else?" the eunuch asked. So Philip explained this scripture and used many others to tell him about the Messiah. As they traveled along, they passed a small oasis and the eunuch said, "See, here is water. Why can't I be baptized?" "If you believe with all your heart, you can," answered Philip. And the eunuch replied, "I believe that Jesus Christ is the Son of God." He stopped the chariot, they went down into the water, and Philip baptized him. When they came up out of the water, the Spirit of the Lord came upon the eunuch, and he went on his way rejoicing.

As the first Ethiopian Christian, the eunuch returned to his homeland to fight the pagan worship of stones, trees, animals, and elemental spirits that had regained acceptance among the Ethiopians. Unfortunately, the task was too great for one man, and there is little indication that any positive results came of his work. If anything, it produced a form of Christianity not unlike some of the Solomonic magic that had existed in Ethiopia since the time of the Queen of Sheba and the Ark of the Covenant, almost a thousand years earlier. The legends of Solomon were clearly well-known in the first century A.D., and in fact, traditional Hebrew, Syrian, Arabic, and Ethiopian sources all agree that King Solomon was a master magician.

SOLOMONIC MAGIC

The underlying theme of magic runs deep within the Ethiopian consciousness, and any "spiritual" man or woman worthy of respect has an understanding of and power over all nature spirits, including the malevolent demons of hell, which they can allegedly "catch in a net like fishes." Throughout history, the Ethiopians have strived to acquire this magic power through the use of amulets, which at one time were made of strips of sheepskin parchment and inscribed with words of power, chants, and incantations. These amulets are worn rolled up around the neck or tied to the left arm. Some inscriptions included the various names of God (Elohim, Jah, El-Shaddai) and other traditional words of power, such as *Lofham* and *Mahfelon*, which were said to have been used by Solomon. In some respects, Ethiopians use their amulets in much the same way Catholics use their rosaries.

As Christianity spread across Ethiopia, this ancient form of magic survived and was adopted by Christians as well. The Ethiopians believed that the greatest of all magicians was Christ, himself, who conquered the devil by fasting for forty days in the desert. Christ gave his apostles a special prayer that, used daily, would save their souls and bodies, deliver them from wrong-thinking, and preserve them from their enemies. Christ's list of enemies included poisons, accidents, physical weakness, intentional evil, curses, blasphemies, ghosts, demons, death, fire, and even the Devil, himself.

Besides this prayer, Christ taught his disciples many other names and words of power. For example, it was said that Christ could scatter demons simply by saying the names *Asparaspes* and *Askoraskis*. However, without the spiritual discipline of prayer and fasting, these words alone were not enough. During Christ's lifetime and in the early days of Christianity, it was believed that all sickness of mind and body were caused by malign spirits. Each fiend had a name and was obliged to obey the greater power that Jesus possessed as the Son of God. This power was passed into his words, and though hidden in the form of parables and teachings, they were in every respect commands that things animate and inanimate were bound to obey. His followers, like their master, admitted that there was magic other than their own in the world. Magicians possessed considerable power to do good as well as harm, but the names and words of power known to Christ were thought to be absolutely invincible. Satan and his devils were rendered powerless when these words were uttered. Whereas the ordinary magicians and sorcerers of Ethiopia had to perform some act or ceremony to produce the desired effect, Christ and those taught by him needed only to utter the name, and their commands were immediately obeyed.

Another example of Christ's power over sorcery comes earlier in the Acts of the Apostles, before the apostle Philip converts the eunuch from Ethiopia. In verses 5–13, it is said that Philip went to Samaria, where a man named Simon had proclaimed himself to be a "great one," by virtue of his miracles and magic. The people of Samaria believed Simon's power to be from God. But when Philip exorcised evil spirits and healed the sick — in the name of Jesus Christ — Simon bowed to this superior power and asked to be baptized. This story of conversion from sorcery to Christianity in Samaria parallels what occurred in Ethiopia: Christianity proved to be more powerful than the local pagan magicians.

Edward Ullendorf in his book *The Ethiopians* traces the roots of magic in the biblical tradition back to the beginning of the Old Testament:

> It is likely that the majority of superstitions and magical practices are derived from the old Cushitic pagan beliefs; yet a very large body of magical craft, contrivances, and prayers were common to most peoples of the ancient Semitic world. There is no doubt that many magical practices were so integral a part of the pagan folklore of Canaan that they were taken over into the Hebrew religion and given a fresh and sublimated significance . . . There is little doubt that the shield of David and the seal of Solomon have a similar origin.[2]

Even after Christianity took hold in Ethiopia, the use of amulets remained popular. Priests have always done lucrative trade in amulets, the most powerful amulet being the cross. But the union of the cross with Solomon's Seal (the star of David) was regarded as the symbol of an especially protective power. It is written on one amulet that the cross wounded the angel of death and the Seal of Solomon compelled the adversary to confess the various means by which he worked his evil, thus revealing his secrets. Other amulets contain partial prayers to the Virgin Mary: "I salute thy sanctuary and its vail." When the inscriptions are lengthy, the amulet often takes the form of a book. In some cases, a very lengthy written work like the *Kebra Nagast* (Glory of the Kings) is considered to be an amulet. The spells or magic prayers on the amulets are usually written in Ge'ez, Ethiopia's ancient ecclesiastical language. They are sometimes ornamented with paintings of the archangels, Michael and Gabriel, or with pictures of Saint George spearing the dragon.

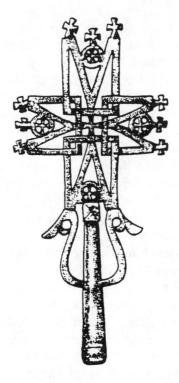

Early bronze processional cross

Many of these superstitious beliefs have been preserved in the West Indian culture, some of which have been incorporated into the modern-day Rastafarian movement. As Christianity moved around the world, it absorbed other native religions rather than denied them. Today, as in the days of Solomon, all spirits are subservient to the most high God as represented through Jesus Christ.

REVEALER OF THE LIGHT

A man named Frumentius, who later became the beloved Saint Abba Salama (meaning revealer of the light), is the person most responsible for bringing orthodox Christianity to Ethiopia as the state religion. Frumentius came to Ethiopia in the fourth century A.D. with his brother Edesius and his uncle Meropious. According to the Roman historian Rufinus, the two young brothers were traveling with their uncle on a trading ship from Tyre, in search of possible trade routes to the Orient. Apparently their ship — having set into port in Ethiopia — was attacked by hostile natives and everyone aboard was put to the sword, except the two young boys. They were spared and taken to the king, whose name was Ella Amida.

Ella Amida took a liking to them and made Edesius his cup-bearer. Frumentius became his secretary, and thereafter they were held in great honor and affection by the king. When King Ella Amida died, leaving his wife with two infant sons — Abreha and Asbeha — as heirs to the throne, the queen begged Frumentius and Edesius to help her with the burden of government until her sons came of age. Frumentius accepted the task and acted as regent for the queen. During this time, God stirred his heart, and Frumentius began to carefully search out Roman merchants who were Christians. Those he found were given great influence at court and urged to establish prayer houses where they might worship. Frumentius encouraged these men by giving them whatever they needed in the way of building materials and land sites. In this way, he prepared the ground for planting the seeds of Christianity in Ethiopia.

When the young princes grew up, they jointly ruled quite harmoniously. In time, however, Abreha emerged as the stronger and more capable ruler of the two, and soon he took the imperial name of Ezana.[3] In the meantime, the two Christian brothers returned to their native Roman Empire. While Edesius went home to visit family and friends, Frumentius met with Queen Helena, the mother of Emperor Constantine. After hearing what he had accomplished in Ethiopia, she urged Frumentius to visit the Coptic Christian Church in Alexandria and ask that a bishop be appointed to administer to the needs of the new Ethiopian Christians. As Frumentius addressed the synod of bishops in Alexandria, the Archbishop Athanasius said to him, "What other man shall be found in whom the spirit of God is so alive as in Frumentius? Who else can accomplish these things?" And with that, Athanasius consecrated Frumentius, who then took the name Abba Salama, revealer of the light. When Abba Salama returned to Axum in 341 A.D., such power and grace had been given to him by God that apostolic miracles were performed and countless number of Ethiopians were converted to the faith.

King Ezana himself had been the first of Frumentius's converts, and he officially declared Christianity as the state religion in

333 A.D. Evidence of this can be seen on the coins from that period. The coins bearing the name of King Ezana changed suddenly from the traditional symbol of the crescent moon and solar disc to the emblem of the cross. The establishment of Christianity as the state religion meant that both the Old and New Testaments had to be translated into the Ethiopian literary language, Ge'ez. Abba Salama had neither the means nor the agents to carry out such a monumental task, and it wasn't until the second half of the fifth century — when large numbers of monks fleeing from persecution by other Christians found refuge in Ethiopia — that this task was undertaken.

THE ETHIOPIAN BIBLE

Before telling the story of what drove these monks to Ethiopia, it would be valuable to look at the Ethiopian version of the Bible as it has been handed down from generation to generation. The Canon of the Ethiopian Bible is made up in the following way. The Old Testament consists of four sections, with a total of forty-six books. The first section contains Mosaic Law, including the following eight books: Genesis, Exodus, Leviticus, Numbers, Deuteronomy, Joshua, Judges, and Ruth.

The second section has the accounts of the kings in the following sixteen books: I Kings (our I Samuel); II Kings (our II Samuel); III Kings (our I Kings); IV Kings (our II Kings); I Ezra (our Esdras); II Ezra (our Nehemiah); I Maccabees; II Maccabees; The Book of Joseph, son of Koryon, otherwise known as III & IV Ezra (or Esdras); I Chronicles; II Chronicles; Job; Psalms; Esther; Judith; and Tobit.

The third section tells about Solomon and contains six books: Proverbs, Wisdom, *Tegsaats* (an Ethiopic word meaning advice), Ecclesiastes, Song of Solomon, and Ecclesiasticus.

And the fourth section deals with the Prophets and includes the following sixteen books: Isaiah, Jeremiah (including Baruch, Lamentations, and Jeremiah's letter to the captive Jews in Babylon), Ezekiel, Daniel, Hosea, Amos, Micah, Joel, Obadiah, Jonah, Nahum, Habakkuk, Zephaniah, Haggai, Zachariah, and Malachi.

There is another book, The Ascension of Isaiah — which is not included in the Western Bible — that tells of Isaiah's vision and his martyrdom. The Ethiopian Bible is the only Bible in the world in which this entire book is preserved. Also exclusive to the Ethiopian Bible is the Book of Enoch, which reveals a great deal about Jewish thinking prior to the birth of Christ, and the Book of Jubilees, which divides all time since creation into periods of forty-nine years.

According to varying sources, the Ethiopian New Testament contains between twenty-seven and thirty-five books. In addition to the standard gospel of twenty books, there are additional works: the Shepherd of Hermes, the Miracles of our Lord Jesus Christ, the Miracles of the Blessed Virgin Mary, the Contendings of the Apostles, and a great deal more information that Haile Selassie became familiar with during the course of his spiritual education. Only during the twentieth century has this information come to the attention of the rest of the Christian world.

However, at the time these holy words were translated, certain theological differences had arisen among the various Christian churches during the early centuries after Christ that created irreparable schisms between the opposing sides. In an attempt to resolve their ideological differences, the ecumenical councils were inaugurated as a forum for discussion. The word *ecumenical* comes from the Greek word meaning the inhabited world. So, the ecumenical council was one in which, ideally, all the churches of the world were represented; the theory being that, with all the churches represented, the Holy Spirit would guide them to infallible conclusions. In reality, there never was a genuine ecumenical council. In 325 A.D., at the Council of Nicea, only the Eastern Christians, represented by the Byzantine church, had a large representation. Nevertheless, there is a readiness today to grant the status of ecumenicality to the Council of Nicea and to the six other councils that followed, which have determined the fundamentals of Christian doctrine ever since.

MONOPHYSITISM: THE DIVINE WITHIN

Next to Nicea, the most important of these was the Council of Chalcedon. This council explicitly defined the Christian doctrine that two natures — one divine and the other human — completely united in Jesus to form one person, who was at the same time God and man. The belief was that only Jesus Christ was capable of this phenomenon. This declaration was accepted by the entire council with the exception of the Monophysite churches. As their root name *mono* indicates, the Monophysites believe that, rather than two separate divine and human natures joining to form one being, there is but one nature in which human and divine are indistinguishable, and that *any* human being is capable of such union. According to the Monophysites, this divine connection to God is *not* exclusive to Jesus Christ, but is available to all true believers. This theological issue — though subtle — was important because rejection of the council's conclusions meant certain persecution. It was from this persecution that the Monophysites fled first to the Coptic Church of Egypt and, later, farther south into Ethiopia. These monks, who eventually arrived in Ethiopia, are responsible for completing the great task of translating the holy scriptures into the Ethiopian language of Ge'ez.

Among the monks who fled to Ethiopia were the famous Nine Saints: Abba Aleph, Abba Sehma, Abba Aragawi, Abba Afse, Abba Garima, Abba Pantalewon, Abba Likanos, Abba Guba, and Abba Yemata. Each of these great ascetics started a monastery in northern Ethiopia, and it is specifically to them that we must credit the translation of the Ethiopic manuscripts. Not all the refugee monks were Monophysite; many were Gnostic and, therefore, didn't identify the church in terms of its ecclesiastical organization. Gnostics believed the true church was invisible and only its members perceived who belonged to it and who didn't. This Gnostic concept of a spiritual church was rejected by the orthodox leaders of the Monophysite sect who instead attempted to construct a universal church, a church open to everyone from every social class and every racial or social origin, whether educated or illiterate. Everyone, in fact, who would submit to their system of organization was welcome to join.

PRAYER AND FASTING

But by the fourth century, many orthodox Christians were adopting Gnostic forms of self-discipline, seeking spiritual insights through solitude. In fact, the terms *monk* and *monastic* come from the Greek word *monachos*, meaning solitary or single. Rather than exclude the monastic movement, the orthodox church moved to bring the monks into line with episcopal authority.

With the growth of the monastic system in Ethiopia came a new emphasis on the practice of fasting. Even today's Ethiopian Christian fasts are frequent and strictly observed, although no one fasts on the Sabbath or during the fifty days between Easter and Pentecost. Under the guidance of the monks, fasting is still used as a form of direct prayer. Fasting is mentioned throughout the Bible; King David fasted before King Solomon was conceived, and Moses received the Covenant after two forty-day fasts at the top of the mountain. When he came down the second time, carrying the tablets that would establish Mosaic Law, Moses' face glowed so much that the people were afraid of him. Jehosephat called on everybody in Judah to fast when he received the news of an enemy's approach, and afterward God caused the attacking armies to turn on each other, thus destroying themselves. The prophet, Ezra, declared a fast at the Ahava River so that all the assembled clans might humble themselves before God. Esther required all the Jews of Shushan to fast with her for three days so that she would receive the Lord's grace. Whenever the Jewish nation wished to unify itself, a three-day fast was planned. In Joel 2:12-15, the spiritual aspirant is advised to cleanse through fasting when the days of tribulation are at hand.

Especially among the Gnostics, the practice of fasting was regarded as a private matter. In the New Testament, Jesus fasted for forty days in the wilderness and overcame the temptations of Satan; but he warned about fasting publicly, "Let no one suspect that you are hungry, and God will reward you." In fact, the element of secrecy in the Gnostic practice of early Christianity centered around the practice of fasting. Those who were ready for this discipline began immediately. For the most part, the greater mass of the population emerging from paganism was introduced to Christianity through festivals. These festivals ultimately became an opportunity to experience conversion of the flesh through prayer and fasting. As new initiates were drawn into the group, they were united with Jesus by Experiencing the Holy Spirit, a spirit greater than all others. Ideologically, the body of the Christian becomes part of the body of the Messiah, who lives and acts through all believers.

However, these Christian festivals have slowly been eroded by Western society and have become times of feasting rather than fasting. In spite of this, Ethiopian Christians — probably due to their isolation from Europe — still practice the ancient law of fasting. They fast on Wednesday and Friday every week, and during the forty days of Lent, until the Sabbath of the Passion. Even this is preceded by the fast of Heraclius, as well as a fast during the

Holy Week of Michelmas, or Christmas. They also observe the Nineveh fast, which occurs during three days in February. In the throes of decadence, the ancient city of Nineveh, capital of Ur (in Mesopotamia), saved itself from destruction through fasting. Having heeded the prophecy of Jonah, everyone from the kings to the lowest servant observed the fast, persuading God to abandon his plans to destroy them.

Other fasts the Ethiopians observe are: the Advent fast, the fast of the Apostles, the fast of the Assumption, the fast of Kueskuan, and the vigil of the Epiphany, at which time they do not even sleep. Added together, these periods of fasting total more than one-third of the year. Although fasting has always been a part of the Solomonic teaching of Jah-weh, the Christian fasting that has been adapted by the Ethiopians is much more strenuous.

Elsewhere in Christendom, the new religion became institutionalized and integrated with the politics of a more worldly existence, and the zeal of the early Christians rapidly diminished. The power of the spirit as an eclectic group gathering in the name of Christ became more and more rare. Individual prophets continued to flourish, but they ran into trouble with the growing church organization, and were often excommunicated for their beliefs. Much of Christian worship was reduced to lip service, and the teachings of Saint Paul became more important than Christ's original message. This led to a form of Christianity based on Saint Paul's intellectualizations, in which Christ was used as an argument and looked upon more as a philosophy than as a spiritual discipline. This new wave of thought created the foundation for an organization in which church and state worked jointly. The organization became known as the Roman Catholic Church. Their domain was the nebulous Holy Roman Empire and incorporated most of Europe. In retrospect, we can only wonder whether Christianity would ever have become so firmly established had Saint Paul's radical point of view not been so readily accepted.

With the exception of Saint Paul, it was the persecution of the early Christian martyrs that probably helped to spread Christian doctrine over much of the known world. Before the time of Saint Paul, those who followed Jesus were thought of as nothing more than a sect of Judaism, just as the first Buddhists were considered a sect of Hinduism. To the outsider, there was nothing startling or revolutionary in the appearance of one more sect. After all, Judaism had survived many divisions, and its laws had withstood

LOS GATOS H.S. LIBRARY

many interpretations. But the doctrine of Jesus — after his death and resurrection — was completely rejected by the Jews. Only when the convert Paul turned away from the indifferent Jewish population and began his fanatic but inspired proselytizing among the Gentiles did the new religion take hold in many of the countries surrounding the Mediterranean Sea.

In Ethiopia, Christianity was settling into an isolation almost as complete as that of the ancient Incas of Peru. During medieval times the world witnessed the rise of Islam and the subsequent struggle between the followers of Christ and the followers of Mohammed. To the Moslems this struggle was the *jihad* or holy war, and to the Christians it was the Crusades. These holy wars occupied much of the political mentality and energy of the nations involved, including western and eastern Europe and the countries of the Middle East.

Fortunately, Ethiopia was spared this devastating conflict because of its unique geography. When the Moslem invaders tried to assault the Christian strongholds in the mountains, the camels — the sole means of military transport for them — died on the cooler, higher plateaus of the Ethiopian highlands. Christianity and the Ethiopian state survived virtually intact, surrounded by the Moslem world, for the next nine hundred years. This created a timeless environment for the young religion to grow, uninfluenced by the politics of the rest of the world. For this reason, Ethiopian Christianity managed to preserve many rare, original documents and is perhaps the purest version of early Christianity still existing on Earth. These are the roots from which the Rastafarians, who emulate many of the old Judeo-Christian practices and traditions, have built their religion.

LALIBELA: ARCHITECT OF ONE OF
THE SEVEN WONDERS OF THE WORLD

Within this Ethiopian isolation, many miraculous events took place, not the least of which was the life of the amazing Lalibela, who lived during the twelfth century (1170–1220 A.D.). From the Ethiopian Royal Chronicles we learn that Lalibela was the son of an aristocrat named Djan (chief or king) Sheyum. After his birth a large swarm of bees surrounded Lalibela. When his mother saw this, the spirit of prophecy came upon her, and she cried out, "The bees know that this child is King." She named him Lalibela, which means the bees recognize his sovereignty, although his brother, Harbay, was the reigning king.

> When Lalibela's brother heard about the prophecy, he became jealous and began to persecute his younger brother. As Lalibela grew up, he became spiritually inclined. He was described as 'without spot or blemish or physical defect of any kind. His cheeks were red like pomegranates, his eyes were like the morning star, his hands were well-shaped, his nose was straight, his mouth was admirable, his speech was eloquent and his voice soft and agreeable. His mental and spiritual qualities matched his physical form, for he was full of wisdom and understanding, pure in spirit, and he was shrewd and cautious in judgment.'[4]

The fearful King Harbay had genuine cause for concern. A group of Harbay's conspirators administered a dose of poison to Lalibela, but he somehow managed to overcome its ill effects. Realizing that the poison was intentionally given to him, Lalibela grieved that his own family would try to kill him. Soon after this incident, angels came to Lalibela and commanded him to build ten monolithic churches, giving him detailed instructions for their dimensions and color. Immediately after the angels' visit, which revealed to him the mysteries of the seven heavens, his family and their friends renewed their persecution. Lalibela was forced to retreat to the desert, where he adopted the life of an ascetic.

While Lalibela was in the desert, he experienced another vision of angels announcing that a Christian maiden chosen by God would come to him to be his wife. At first Lalibela refused to accept this and agreed to marry her only after the angels reminded him that it was his duty to obey God's will. Soon after this, Lalibela's enemies made false accusations to the king, alleging that Lalibela had married a woman who had been promised to another. Hearing this, the king gave the order to have Lalibela whipped. The king's men took turns flogging Lalibela, while the king was in church receiving his sacrament. Miraculously, Lalibela survived this beating and, with his wife, returned to the desert. Some time after that incident, an angel again appeared and instructed Lalibela to go back to the capital. This time King Harbay met his brother repentently, and because of divine intervention, he abdicated the throne in Lalibela's favor.

The time had come for Lalibela to fulfill God's command to build the ten monolithic churches, and he devoted himself to this new work with great enthusiasm. Lalibela collected artists, carpenters, masons, and other craftsmen. He had tools forged and arranged a scale of wages for the workers. It is said that the angels worked alongside the mortals and, during the night, doubled what the workers had done during the day. When the churches were finished, Lalibela felt that his work in this world was complete. He had no wish to continue his personal reign, and he did not want his descendants to succeed him because he believed the time had come for sovereignty to be restored to the Solomonic line. He distributed his goods among the poor and, shortly thereafter, fell sick and died, drawing to a conclusion the Zagwé dynasty in Ethiopia.

The Zagwés officially abdicated the throne almost sixty years later, 1268 A.D., under the rule of Nakueto Laab, the nephew of Lalibela. With the persuasion of the powerful Abuna (archbishop) Takla Haymanot, the monarchy was restored to the original royal line by Yekuno Amlak. In recompense for his efforts, the abuna received one-third of the kingdom as a land grant for the church. Lalibela's precedent made it possible for successive generations, including His Majesty Haile Selassie, to claim genuine Solomonic descent.

The amazing rock-hewn churches can still be seen today and are now considered one of the seven wonders of the ancient world. They were originally built in the ancient city of Roha in the region of Lasta, which has been renamed Lalibela in modern times. Carved from one piece of living rock, "all who have seen them marvel, not only at their beauty, but at the mind of the man who conceived their design and the colossal labor which was expended in their making."[5] These cave-like churches encouraged musical experiments using the acoustical effects of the echo, and this flavor can clearly be heard in contemporary Rastafarian, or reggae, music. This musical form of worship dates back to the time of King David of Israel, who was famous for playing the harp and who led dances around the Ark of the Covenant.

THE THREAT OF ISLAM

Like an island in a sea of Islam, Ethiopian Christianity remained untouched until the Portuguese missionaries arrived between 1521 and 1526. Father Francisco Alvarez — who resembled the Jesuit missionary depicted in the *Shogun* story of Japan in the sixteenth century — traveled extensively throughout Ethiopia, perhaps in search of the legendary Christian king, Prester John.

It is speculated that Prester John could have been enthroned in the eighth century A.D. by Ogier The Dane, who left a Christian king in Abyssinia after conquering the fourteen Abyssinian provinces for their gold. The name John could also be a corruption of the Ethiopian title, *djan*, which means chief or king. Prester Djan could also have been Delnaad, a Christian prince, whose descendant restored the Solomonic line in 1258 A.D. through Takla Haymanot.

In any case, Alvarez mentioned in a diary of his journey that he saw the church of the Virgin Mary in Axum, twelve hundred years after its construction by Abba Salama in 341 A.D. This centuries-old church was constructed on the site of an even more ancient holy place, the temple of the Queen of Sheba. Tragically, several years after Father Alvarez's account, Moslem invaders destroyed the church. It was rebuilt in the sixteenth century on a less grand scale and is now known as the Church of Saint Mary of Axum.

Ironically, it was fortunate for the Ethiopians that the Portuguese befriended them. Bermudez, the one man who stayed behind in Ethiopia after the rest of the Portuguese missionaries returned home in 1526, somehow managed to be appointed as the abuna and, subsequently, to solicit Portuguese intervention in Ethiopia. The threat to Ethiopia began in 1527 when the infamous Moslem invader, Gran the Left-Handed, armed with guns and cannons, overran the country. "The very existence of Ethiopia was threatened, the land was laid waste, churches were destroyed, ancient manuscripts were burned, the priests were slain and utter ruin seemed imminent."[6] Probably with the hope of aiding the legendary Prester John, King John II of Portugal agreed to send a party of soldiers under the capable leadership of Christopher de Gama. The small army landed successfully at Massawa in 1541, and by 1544 the Moslem army was defeated. Gran was finally killed at a battle near Lake Tana, at the headwaters of the Nile; and Ethiopia was saved.

But the Ethiopian Christians paid a heavy price for their rescue. Those Jesuit missionaries who remained in Ethiopia embarked on a full-scale campaign to convert the Coptic Christians to Roman Catholics. Father Pero Paéz, a sincere and gentle Jesuit, succeeded in converting King Susenyos to the Catholic faith in 1621.

After the death of Paéz, a man named Mendez took the seat of Jesuit power. In contrast to his predecessor, Mendez was a cold, exacting, and brutal man who persuaded Susenyos to persecute his own people if they did not convert to the doctrine of the Europeans. Not only was the Monophysite belief considered to be heresy, it was forbidden to practice circumcision or observe the Sabbath on a Saturday, both of which the Coptic Christians were accustomed to doing. Naturally, there was tremendous popular resistance that eventually erupted into civil war. During one single battle, King Susenyos massacred eight thousand of his own countrymen. The crown prince, Fasiladas, said to his father, "The men you see laying dead here were neither pagans nor Moslems over whose death we would rejoice, but Christians, your subjects and fellow countrymen, and some of them were your relations. It is not victory that we have gained, for we have driven our swords into our own bodies." Fasiladas's words reached deep into Susenyos's heart. The king renounced his conversion to Catholicism and abdicated the throne in favor of his son.

The new king, who reigned from 1632–1665 A.D., predictably banished the Jesuit missionaries in 1633, and forbade them ever to return. This experience planted a seed of mistrust and suspicion of foreigners, especially Europeans, in the minds of the Ethiopian people, an attitude that has survived into the twentieth century. Self-serving Europeans' intervention in the affairs of the Ethiopians became a familiar theme during the reign of Haile Selassie, whose life will be explored in greater depth in the following chapters.

For the next several hundred years (1665–1889), the centralized monarchy of Ethiopia slowly deteriorated into provincial rule of the fourteen provinces in Ethiopia by the local *rases*, or lords. The struggle for power ensued among the Shoan aristocrats (the feudal ruling class of provincial rases) and continued for generations, until the consolidation of Menelik II's power in 1889. Menelik II succeeded Emperor Yohannes IV (John) to the throne. He reestablished Ethiopia as a unified state and set a precedent for the rule of Haile Selassie, which would usher in the twentieth century to this ancient feudal society.

[1] Not to be confused with the Candace queens of Meroe.
[2] Edward Ullendorf, *The Ethiopians*, p. 103.

[3]This is a common practice in Ethiopia. For example, Ras Tafari took the name Haile Selassie when he became emperor.

[4]Sir E.A. Wallis Budge, *History of Ethiopia*, pp. 164–165.

[5]*Ibid.*, p. 280.

[6]Stuart Bergsma, *Rainbow Empire*, p. 211.

4

The Ascent to Power

During a torrential thunderstorm at his summer residence in the mountains, Ras (meaning lord or prince; like *rajah* in India) Makonnen welcomed his long-awaited baby son into the world. Tafari Makonnen was born at approximately 12:00 noon on July 23, 1892. In a land where rain is always welcome, the thunderstorm was considered a good omen. There was great rejoicing because Ras Makonnen, then governor of the wealthy province of Harar, finally had an heir. At the baby's christening, Emperor Menelik II sent many gifts to the child who would one day take his place on the throne. However, the ascent to power for Ras Tafari was not to be easy. Instead, destiny gave him a treacherous path to follow, full of unanticipated detours, challenges, and compromises. Had the throne simply been handed to him, as was hinted at the time of his birth and more clearly indicated later in his childhood, perhaps Haile Selassie I would not have had the opportunity to learn such valuable lessons about life. The taste of betrayal, defeat, and human injustice served to make his accomplishments more valued and his ethical posture more of an example for others, whether they be Rastafarians, Christians, Ethiopians, or simply human beings.

RAS TAFARI'S CHILDHOOD

Ras Makonnen, Tafari's father, was perhaps the single most important figure in the future emperor's life. After the death of his mother, Waizero Yeshimabeit, during childbirth two years later, Tafari relied solely on his father for guidance. Ras Makonnen was a popular governor. He had won over the hearts of the Hararis after conquering the tyrannical Emirs who had governed the province before him. Having been exposed to a more developed civilization during a visit to Rome, Ras Makonnen recognized the need to bring Ethiopia into the twentieth century. He returned to upgrade the sanitary conditions of his people and open the first hospital in Ethiopia. Ras Makonnen demonstrated the insight and humanitarian consciousness that his son would emulate in future years.

Ras Makonnen was also a fierce warrior. During a decisive battle against the Italians in 1896, Ras Makonnen successfully lay siege to the town of Magdala (Makalle) and defeated the European invaders as they crossed the Eritrean border at Adowa. The humiliation of the Italian troops, who were subsequently emasculated by the barbaric Galla tribesmen, would later serve as fuel for revenge. With this victory, however, the bond between Ras Makonnen and Emperor Menelik II became thicker than the family blood that already united them.[1] Menelik's power over the fuedal rases of Ethiopia was consolidated, and Ras Makonnen became his most trusted aid. Under Menelik II, the nation's capital became *Addis Ababa*, meaning new flower, although at the time it was not much more than a cluster of mud huts.

Young Tafari had a visionary mind. At the age of seven, he had a premonition that he would one day be the king of kings. He was an avid student and hungered for any books he could find on the subject of Ethiopian history. He memorized all the folklore, especially the story of the illustrious union of King Solomon and the Queen of Sheba, his ancestors. Many of his tutors were European missionaries, and by the age of eleven, Tafari could converse in fluent French with his tutor, Aba Samuel. Shortly after Tafari's father returned from the coronation of King Edward VII in England, Menelik II summoned both father and son to his court in Addis Ababa. Although it was the first long journey of Tafari's life – an eighteen-day trek through rugged, mountainous terrain by mule caravan – by this time, Tafari had already shot his first lion and captured his own wild pony. The emperor was greatly impressed by the young prince's knowledge and poise, and in 1905, when he was thirteen, Tafari received the title of *Dejazmach*, the equivalent of High Sheriff. Ras Makonnen officially proclaimed Tafari as his heir, an important step because everyone expected Ras Makonnen to be named as Menelik's successor. As his father's heir, that meant Tafari would eventually inherit the throne. This prospect was very disturbing to Empress Taitu, who had ambitions of her own. This turn of events was not applauded by Ras Mikael either, for he had married one of Menelik's daughters and wanted to see his own son, Lij Yasu, rise to power.

THE STRUGGLE FOR POWER

In April of the following year, Ras Makonnen was taken ill at his estate in Harar, and while on his way to Addis Ababa at the request of the emperor, Tafari's father suddenly died. This was a great tragedy for the promising young Tafari, who was suddenly alone in the world. He was only fourteen and had to survive in a hierarchy that regarded him as a threat. The sudden death of Ras Makonnen, who was normally a robust and healthy man, could only be viewed with an eye of suspicion, and its convenience to his opponents at court could not be overlooked. Nevertheless, it seemed certain that Tafari would at least inherit the province of Harar and be given the title *ras*. At that same time, another unfortunate coincidence for Tafari occurred: Menelik II began to suffer a series of strokes that would eventually incapacitate him. Empress Taitu assumed more and more of the decision-making power and gave the governorship of Harar to Tafari's older half-brother, Yilma. However, the excuse that Tafari was too young was considered lame by the emperor, and as soon as Menelik recovered temporarily from his illness, the young Tafari was summoned to live at court with the aging king.

Menelik sensed the danger Tafari was in and wanted to give him both protection and an education in kingship. The few years these two had together were invaluable, and as long as Menelik was alive, Tafari was safe from harm. Menelik gave him the small, faraway province of Somali with which to practice his skills of government and to learn what imperial survival was all about. The year was 1906.

Tafari soon became accustomed to the pomp and ritual of

court life. The royal lifestyle also included strict observance of religious fasts, which account for 180 days out of the year. The Ethiopian Church upholds the practice of fasting (which requires abstinence from all animal food, and no food or drink whatsoever at Easter), more than any other church in the world. Tafari took to this practice rather naturally, and it strengthened rather than weakened him. In contrast, his adversary, Lij Yasu, would smuggle in pieces of raw flesh to chew during the long, traditional church services. Tafari actually found the days of feasting more difficult than the days of fasting. He was also reluctant and shy with concubines, preferring the company of one woman, to whom he was faithful all his life. This was quite unusual in Ethiopian society.

Tafari possessed another invaluable quality, patience. He had the ability to wait like a cat for his moment to strike. He also restrained himself from costly impulsive and emotional reactions, which more than once saved his life. He was able to recognize when to flee those situations that would otherwise result in his premature and unnecessary death; he saw no virtue in becoming a martyr to a cause he had not yet had the opportunity to promote. Tafari could control his temper much better than his mentor, Menelik (who would often become enraged when things did not please him), and he developed a regal silence and icy stare to express his displeasure. Tafari learned to maintain his dignity even in the face of bitter and humiliating disappointments, a quality he had the chance to demonstrate on a number of occasions in his lifetime. These qualities made him stand out in a court ruled by excessive pleasures, ruthless ambition, and personal greed.

Within a few years, Menelik's faculties had so deteriorated that he was barely able to speak. The once proud king had become merely a paralyzed figurehead propped up on pillows. Queen Taitu had her relatives nominated to positions of power, and Menelik's thirteen-year-old grandson, Lij Yasu, was named as successor to the throne. He could hardly wait for the old man to die. At sixteen, Tafari was again denied the province of Harar after the death of his half-brother Yilma. Locked away helplessly behind closed doors, Menelik was unavailable to plead Tafari's case. Queen Taitu, anxious to send Tafari to the far reaches of the empire, gave him control of the small province of Sidamo upon his eighteenth birthday. It was actually in Tafari's best interest that he was removed from court; had he been named as Menelik's successor, there is a chance that he would have become a casualty in the struggle for power that ensued shortly thereafter.

By 1912, Lij Yasu had consolidated his position in Addis Ababa and granted his cousin the inheritance that was his due. After eighteen months in Sidamo, Tafari finally became governor of Harar, in return for which Lij Yasu extracted an oath of loyalty. Since the time of Ras Makonnen, Harar had experienced great exploitation at the hands of its rulers. Extensive restoration was needed, and Tafari, now nearly twenty, seemed equal to the task.

Lij Yasu also gave Tafari a wife, Waizero Menen, with whom Tafari had fallen deeply in love. Since Menen was his niece, Lij Yasu audaciously assumed that he had the right to give her away, in spite of the fact that she was already married.

In Ethiopia, marriage is somewhat more casual and less binding than in Western society; either party can be divorced simply by making a statement to a public official. As a result Ethiopian nobility usually married many times for either convenience or political ends. Dynastic marriages were commonplace, even more so than in Europe, since vows could be so easily dissolved according to the changing tide of events. However, church marriages sanctified by the abuna (archbishop) were commitments for life. Although Menen had run away from her husband, he was nonetheless determined to get her back. So Tafari made arrangements with the abuna to marry Menen, and the ceremony was carried out before her ex-husband had a chance to intervene.

THE REIGN OF LIJ YASU

The reign of Lij Yasu was a mockery of all that an emperor traditionally represents. The arrogant prince cared more about a fresh supply of women, an abundance of *tej* (Ethiopian wine), and raw meat than he did about the welfare of his country or its inhabitants. He considered all of Ethiopia's resources to exist solely for his personal pleasure; he was a malevolent despot with a chronic case of syphilis. Lij Yasu could easily be compared to the perverse Roman emperor Caligula, for his lack of ethics and degenerate standards of behavior. He tortured, massacred, and raped his people, and he enslaved them by the thousands. During his five years in power (1911–1916), Lij Yasu managed to nearly destroy the unity that Menelik had painstakingly created during his reign. So desperate was Ehiopia's need to be rid of this one-man plague, that Tafari was literally driven to betray his oath of loyalty to his cousin.

The hollow shell of the man who had once been the great Emperor Menelik II finally died on December 12, 1912. Ras Mikael, Yasu's father, made plans to have Yasu officially crowned as emperor in 1914. The coronation was a hoax set up only to bring together all of Yasu's relatives and political enemies so that they could be banished to some inaccessible mountaintop. Fortunately, Tafari had been forewarned not to attend. Tafari was very tolerant of his cousin and chose to bide his time until the moment was ripe for a coup d'état.

What finally spurred Tafari to take action was Lij Yasu's conversion to Islam. Tafari could not sit back and watch his cousin simply hand Ethiopia, one of the oldest Christian nations on earth, over to the Moslems. Ethiopia had successfully resisted Islam for centuries, and Tafari was determined to see that his country remained a Christian state.

With the arrival of their second child imminent, Tafari had to leave Menen in Harar when he traveled to Addis Ababa in answer to a call from the Council of Ministers. He reluctantly abandoned Harar to the power of the Moslem Party, due to the greater peril of Ethiopia. Ignoring the warnings of the Ethiopian Church, Lij Yasu was making plans for the direct Islamization of the entire country. Even the British troops in nearby Somali were ready to support the fall of Lij Yasu and the rise of a new emperor. The British Foreign Office sent an ultimatum to Lij Yasu with four demands that essentially insisted he retract the political power and influence that he had given to his Moslem friends. The note was coolly ignored. By this time, Menen was in labor, but Tafari was denied permission to leave Addis Ababa. He was a virtual prisoner and was forced to celebrate the birth of his first son with the soldiers that surrounded him. Now that he had an heir, Tafari was an even greater threat to Lij Yasu.

In the meantime, Lij Yasu slipped away to visit Harar with Menen's ex-husband Lul Seged, who expected to repossess her as his wife. The situation was very tense, and from Addis Ababa, Tafari felt helplessly unable to protect his wife and baby son. However, he was able to arrange for a trusted friend to smuggle Menen and the child, disguised as peasants, out of the city, a ruse that was carried out just minutes before Yasu and Lul Seged stormed into Tafari's home.

In Addis Ababa, Tafari rallied the priesthood and the majority of the Council of Ministers to his side. Further, he succeeded in persuading the hesitant abuna that it was time to excommunicate the emperor. Ras Tafari went so far as to have leaflets, denouncing Lij Yasu and inciting rebellion, dropped from the sky by aircraft. But, just as victory seemed near, a thunderstorm soaked the pamphlets, and the attempted coup was aborted. Lij Yasu assured himself that his power remained firmly intact.

The next time, Tafari's plans were more secretive and better prepared. The troops of three of his closest allies were stationed in defense against the wrath of Ras Mikael (Yasu's father), who was sure to retaliate. Tafari then gained control of the council through a coalition with the Shoan chiefs and had a proclamation denouncing Yasu awaiting the chief minister and the abuna. The abuna was forced to release all of them from their oath of loyalty to the emperor, and Tafari was finally successful in overthrowing Yasu, although the price for victory was high. Due to the essential alliance with the Shoan chiefs, who regarded the energetic young Tafari with a conservative eye, Tafari did not become emperor as everyone had anticipated. Instead, he became regent for Empress Zauditu, Menelik's daughter and Queen Taitu's puppet. It must have been a deep disappointment for Tafari, whose influence and maneuvering had engineered the rebellion. He had to wait another fourteen years before assuming the title he so rightly deserved.

FROM REGENT TO EMPEROR

The Council of Ministers, comprised mainly of aristocratic Shoan chiefs, was reluctant to put Tafari on the throne because of his enthusiasm for sweeping reform. The Ethiopian rases maintained their wealth and political power through an outdated feudal system, which Tafari was determined to do away with. Like his father, Tafari dreamed of bringing Ethiopia into the twentieth century and building a strong centralized government. He wanted to abolish slavery, to centralize taxation, to establish a national army, to build schools and universities, and to construct hospitals, roads, air transport, communications networks, and more. Reflective of the deeply-rooted Ethiopian mistrust for anything and anyone foreign (the word *ferengi* [foreign] has negative connotations for most Ethiopians), these modern ideas were not enthusiastically received because they were seen as the European way of life.

Despite the apprehensions of the council, Tafari was given the title *ras* and officially became heir to the throne. He had finally achieved, at the age of twenty-four, what had eluded him ten years earlier.

While the rest of the world fought World War I, Ethiopia attempted to maintain some degree of stability with the shaky coalition of rases being held together by Regent Ras Tafari. Acting as regent for Empress Zauditu, Ras Tafari played a cat-and-mouse game with the elusive Lij Yasu. With Yasu still at large, Ras Tafari's range of political freedom was limited. Eventually, Yasu was captured and kept as a comfortable prisoner under the watchful eye of one of Ras Tafari's allies.

But then old Queen Taitu tried to move back into the palace and usurp Ras Tafari's position. He outsmarted her by luring Ras Gugsa — Zauditu's husband and Taitu's nephew — out of the palace following a drunken orgy and never allowing him to return. Without Ras Gugsa, Empress Zauditu and Queen Taitu were powerless. As cruel as it may seem to separate husband and wife, the separation was necessary to avoid another struggle for power and an unwanted heir to the throne. Ras Tafari quietly informed the empress that she was divorced and would, from that time on, devote all of her attention to her new husband, Ethiopia. It was soon said of the leader, "Do not underestimate the power of Tafari. He creeps like a mouse, but has the jaws of a lion."[2] This was, in fact, the very image that young Tafari had worked so long and hard to develop.

By 1918, many of Ras Tafari's enemies were rendered harmless, and he sought to enter Ethiopia into the arena of world politics. After World War I, the desire for a world organization that would preserve and promote world peace was intense. It was in this vein that the League of Nations was established. In 1923, Ras Tafari applied for Ethiopia's admission to the League, a move that would later bring about a great moment in world history.

In October 1928, the last of Empress Zauditu's allies had died, leaving her impotent. Ras Tafari became Negus Tafari Makonnen, or king, and the coalition of feudal rases was on its way out. Even the new abuna from Alexandria promised to stay out of political affairs. Only one obstacle stood in Tafari's path before he could assume the position of king of kings. Ras Gugsa, Zauditu's husband, had mustered an army to march on Addis Ababa in an attempt to overthrow Tafari and restore his wife to power. Ras

Tafari's intelligence system kept him informed of the conspirators' progress, and at a well-chosen moment, an airplane dropped the first bombshells ever to fall on Ethiopian soil. Caught by surprise, the army of rebels scattered in every direction. Ras Gugsa died in battle, followed two days later by the death of his heartbroken wife, Empress Zauditu, who reportedly refused to end her Lenten fast. Actual details of her death were not released.

By April 1930, the way was clear for Ras Tafari to fulfill his long-awaited destiny, and on November 2, 1930, Ras Tafari was crowned His Imperial Majesty, Haile Selassie I, Conquering Lion of the Tribe of Judah, Elect of God, King of Kings, Lord of Lords, Emperor of Ethiopia.

[1] Ras Makonnen was the son of Menelik's sister Tanana.
[2] Leonard O. Mosley, *The Conquering Lion*, p. 135.

5

The Lion of Judah

Wearing the crown of emperor, Haile Selassie immediately began laying the foundation that would bring Ethiopia out of feudal isolation and into the twentieth century. Ras Tafari's great foresight in applying for Ethiopia's admission into the League of Nations in 1923 necessitated abolishment of slavery in 1924 to conform to the league's standards on human rights. But before he could accomplish more in his modernization plans, he was forced to contend with the imperialistic ambitions of yet another European power.

Italy's designs on Ethiopia reached as far back as 1869, the year the Suez Canal opened. Once the Red Sea became an international waterway, many European powers became suddenly interested in the lands that lay along its shores. In 1869, a private Italian company bought the entire Red Sea port of Assab from the local ruling ras, thus establishing Italy's entry into Ethiopian territory.

In 1885, Italy took its first aggressive action and occupied the port of Massawa, 275 miles to the north. This led to armed conflict with the Ethiopians, and the Italians were seriously defeated at Dogali in 1887. Trying a different approach, the Italians attempted psychological warfare, pitting the local rases against each other. Menelik II, then only a ras, accepted Italian gifts of arms and

The Bettman Archive

His Imperial Majesty Haile Selassie I, King of Kings, Lord of Lords,
Conquering Lion of the Tribe of Judah, Elect of God, Emperor of Ethiopia

munitions with the hope of overthrowing his rival, Emperor Yohannes IV (John). The Italians promised to make him emperor if he was successful in the coup; however, Menelik never instituted his plan because Emperor Yohannes was killed in battle only a year later. In 1889 — without the stain of bloodshed — Menelik was chosen by the Ethiopians to become emperor.

Italy took advantage of the change in government by drawing up the Treaty of Ucciali, certain they could count on Menelik to pay his dues. Two versions of this treaty were actually drawn up, one for the Italians and one for the Ethiopians. The Italian version stated that Ethiopia fell under Italy's protectorate in the arena of world affairs. This meant that Ethiopia had to obtain Italy's approval in any international dealings and could not act independently on foreign policy. The *Amharic* (Ethiopian) version, the only one that was actually signed by Menelik, stated that Ethiopia had the option to call on Italy's assistance in world affairs when deemed necessary by the emperor. The discrepancy over these contrasting interpretations brought about the first serious dispute between Italy and Ethiopia. As a result, Menelik denounced the treaty in 1893, an act which to the Italians meant certain war.

The Italians were already well established in Eritrea, the coastal zone along the Red Sea. After being attacked by 10,000 Ethiopians, led by Emperor John's son, the Italians responded with a new invasion and succeeded in occupying three major towns in northern Ethiopia. At this time, Ras Makonnen, Ras Tafari's father, joined Menelik with 30,000 troops and successfully laid siege to the Italians, who surrendered at Magdala. It was January 1896.

Six weeks later, the Italians suffered their humiliating defeat at Adowa, the sting of which would feed their revenge for years to come. A number of wounded Italians brought back to Massawa by the Red Cross had been emasculated by the local Galla tribesmen. This atrocity is explained by the ancient custom of this savage tribe to prove their manhood by presenting the testicles of an enemy to a prospective bride. Although Menelik was not responsible for this barbarism, he took the blame for it in the eyes of the Italians.

The Italians retreated to Europe, their imperialistic visions crushed. They vowed to take revenge on the Ethiopians, but it wasn't until Benito Mussolini's rise to power in the 1930s that the opportunity arose.

By the 1930s, Italy sought to neutralize the effects of the worldwide Great Depression by arming itself. Needing raw

materials for its growing war industry, Italy once again cast an imperialistic gaze upon Ethiopia. Italy also felt the need to prove itself as a "virile nation" by assuming some colonial territory. As one British historian explains, "She came too late into the nineteenth century scramble for colonies, and owing to an inefficient government, was poorly treated at the Peace Conference of 1918."[1]

Mussolini thought he could achieve his colonial ambitions through sheer superiority and based his actions on the notion that nothing would unite the country better than a successful conquest. Equally important, Mussolini sought to reinforce the Italian belief in the glories of fascism.

Believing that the Ethiopians could be easily manipulated with bribes and coercion, Mussolini ordered the Italian media to spread propaganda about Ethiopia, portraying Ethiopians as a backward, cruel, slave-trading people desperately in need of an Italian civilizing influence.

Since the signing of the Treaty of Friendship in 1928, Mussolini had attempted to use Ras Tafari as a political puppet. In the treaty, the two nations had agreed to share in the building of a road from the coastal port of Assab to Addis Ababa by way of Dessye, near Lalibela, in the east-central region. The Italians agreed to build the first half of the road as far as Dessye, which they did, stipulating that they had easement rights along the full length of the highway to the capitol. Shrewd as he was, Ras Tafari saw that by agreeing to this he would be giving them direct access into the heart of Ethiopia. He backed out of the deal with the Italians and asked the Dutch to finish the road as far as Addis Ababa. Angered by this turn of events, Mussolini superficially proclaimed "friendship" with Ethiopia as late as 1934, while scheming to conquer the country by force.

THE ITALIAN INVASION

On the morning of October 2, 1935, the Italians crossed over into Ethiopia from Eritrea. Haile Selassie had been emperor for only five years. In the capital of Addis Ababa, an emergency meeting of the Council of Ministers was called, at which the emperor addressed his countrymen:

The hour is grave. Arise, each of you. Take up arms and run to the defense of your country. Repel the invader.

May those who are unable, because of weakness and in-
firmity, to take active part in this sacred quarrel, help us
with their prayer. All come forward for your emperor
and for your country.[2]

However, the ill-prepared nature of Ethiopia's regular armed
forces, partially due to the recent civil war, made the contest one in
which Ethiopia never really stood a chance. The Italians had a
modern force of 650,000 men, two million tons of ammunition,
400 war planes (Ethiopia had none), and poison gas. In contrast,
the Ethiopians engaged in hand-to-hand combat, often with
nothing more than cold steel.

In an effort to placate Italy and prevent its political and
military alliance with Hitler in Germany, Britain and France refused to sell arms to the Ethiopians and chose to ignore their proclaimed alliance with Haile Selassie. Until then, the Ethiopians had
relied on the British Foreign Office to intervene on their behalf in
the face of outright aggression. Unaware of the larger political
situation in Europe — which would later culminate in World War
II — the Ethiopians were surprised to find themselves out in the
cold. One could even call the response of the British, as indicated
by their subsequently cool behavior in the League of Nations, a
subtle betrayal. Leonard Mosley, who wrote Emperor Haile
Selassie's biography, describes it as "misplaced faith."

Another crucial factor in the Italians' easy victory was the
treachery of Ras Gugsa, Haile Selassie's son-in-law. Ras Gugsa
was supposed to have led an Ethiopian force of 10,000 to head off
the invaders in the north from Eritrea. Having grown tired of being subservient to his father-in-law, who was unwilling to promote
him, Ras Gugsa was easily seduced by promises of power from the
Italians. On October 5, 1935, only three days after the invasion,
Ras Gugsa cut down the telephone lines between Addis Ababa and
the rest of the Ethiopian army in the north and marched north-
ward to join the Italians rather than fight them.

The traitorous Ras Gugsa also brought over to the Italians a
Swiss engineer who had surveyed the entire highway system in
Ethiopia. The Swiss engineer had in his possession a complete set
of maps that allowed the Italians to see which roads were passable
and where they connected. They used this invaluable information
for the rest of the war.

A description that characterizes the entire war experience for the Ethiopian people was given by Dr. John Melly of the British Ambulance Service.

> This isn't a war — it isn't even slaughter. It's the torture of tens of thousands of defenseless men, women, and children with bombs and poison gas. They're using gas incessantly, and we've treated hundreds of cases, including infants in arms. And the world looks on — and passes by on the other side.[3]

It wasn't long before even the Red Cross withdrew from the grim situation.

Under the leadership of the emperor himself, the Ethiopians battled valiantly for months, fighting the Italians who had made their strongholds in the mountains to the north. Plagued by naive idealism, poor military tactics, and devastating treachery, the natives were completely overwhelmed and the Ethiopian army collapsed in total disorder.

Stunned and bewildered, Haile Selassie left all his possessions to be divided among his scattering forces and retreated to the caves of Lalibela, the rock-hewn churches made holy more than 700 years earlier. In a state of helpless surrender, he fell on his knees before the administering priest. There he fasted and prayed for 48 hours during the Easter weekend, seeking some understanding of what was happening around him. It is likely that his ongoing and close relationship with God renewed his spirit to continue the ordeal. Exhausted, the emperor made his way back to the capital by April 18, 1936, knowing that the Italian occupation of Ethiopia was a *fait accompli*.

With the occupation of Addis Ababa on May 5, 1936, only six months after the initial invasion, the Italian troops under Marshall Badoglio had brought Ethiopia firmly under Italian control. From the balcony of the Palazzio Venezia in Rome, Mussolini proclaimed to a delirious crowd that Ethiopia had been annexed. Fascist Italy had now accomplished what Imperial Rome and the invincible fury of Islam had failed to do. This was the greatest moment of triumph in Mussolini's life. He had avenged Adowa and wiped out the Italians' sense of inferiority.

Haile Selassie had no alternative but to flee the country. The emperor realized that he had only one card left to play, an appeal to the League of Nations. Addis Ababa was evacuated and looted before the arrival of the Italian troops, leaving the enemy little to relish in their victory. The invaders could not even find much to eat, and were forced onto strict rations in order to survive.

At 4:00 a.m. on May 2, 1936, Haile Selassie escaped by train with his family, taking with him his old enemy Ras Hailu, who would have proven very useful to the Italians. The emperor's journey into exile was a painful and humiliating experience for him, one which he accepted with grace and wisdom. His dramatic departure in the middle of the night could not have been more timely as the Italians were only two hours behind him and bent on his demise. The royal family boarded the British *HMS Enterprise* in the port of Djibouti and sailed to Palestine, which was under British mandate. From there Haile Selassie, the Lion of Judah, King of Kings, Elect of God, made plans to address the world through the League of Nations. It was his intention to warn the free world of the growing fascist menace and his hope to rescue his endangered nation.

ADDRESSING THE LEAGUE OF NATIONS

Haile Selassie's welcome to Jerusalem was disgracefully in-hospitable. The British regarded the ex-emperor — as they called him — as a great embarrassment and did not want the Italians to think he had their official endorsement. Haile Selassie sent a tele-gram to the League of Nations on May 10, five days into his exile, not with any genuine hope of repatriation, but with the intention of making a statement to the world about the league's betrayal of Ethiopia in its hour of need. The members of the league realized they had an angry scapegoat on their hands.

Ethiopia's fate was sealed before Haile Selassie spoke at the League of Nations in Geneva on June 30, 1936. England and France had decided to lift sanctions against Italy to appease Mussolini. Nevertheless, the speech was given and its impact was to have a more lasting effect than anything Haile Selassie had ever said, or would ever say again. He gave the world a prophetic warning about the looming fascist menace. He intimated that, although Ethiopia was but a small country in Africa, they should heed the precedent because any of their own countries could be next.

The following scene was reported in the news media of the day:

Wide World Photos, Inc.

Haile Selassie addressing the League of Nations

The atmosphere at Geneva was one of doom and crisis. Into the tense forum Haile Selassie made his entry. He had silently come into the hall where the assembly met, and he sat quietly in the fifth row awaiting his call to speak. He made his way to the rostrum, a small, frail, tired figure in a white tunic and a black cape. As he stood before the microphone, there was a breathless hush, and the eyes of all present were fixed on him. As he was about to speak, the gallery was startled by members of the Italian press[4]

The emperor described the turmoil this way:

When we . . . stood by the lectern, the Italians who had come there for news reporting started to whistle continuously with the intention of obstructing our speech and rendering it inaudible. At this moment, the Romanian delegate Nicola Titulescu remarked to the President of the Assembly, 'For the sake of justice, silence those beasts!'[5]

The President of the Assembly ordered the guards to expel the Italians by force. The dignified emperor then gave his speech. He confronted his audience with the reality of what they were doing, and all present were riveted. Haile Selassie's words would echo in history books for years to come.

> I, Haile Selassie I, am here today to claim that justice which is due my people . . . There is no precedent for a head of state speaking personally in this assembly. But there is also no precedent for a people being victim to such injustice and being at present threatened by abandonment to its aggressor.[6]

After reviewing the military and diplomatic events of the past eight months, the eloquent speaker came to the core of the issue, with an ominous warning.

> The problem submitted to the assembly today is . . . collective security. It is the very existence of the League of Nations . . . God and his history will remember your judgment.[7]

The league was listening to the prophecy of its own doom. Haile Selassie warned that if the league continued to withhold its support for Ethiopia, the Covenant of the league would be worthless and the league would be regarded with contempt by the Axis powers. He called upon the league to enforce Articles 10 and 16 of the Covenant, which guarantee against aggression, stating that the league would take immediate action against the offending country by severing all trade and financial relations. The emperor's deeply moving speech went largely ignored.

Winston Churchill, then only a member of the British Parliament, blamed the Baldwin government for the whole situation. Churchill advanced the theory that had the British prime minister stood behind the emperor, as advised by Anthony Eden, things would have turned out differently. "The fact that the nerve of the British government was not equal to the occasion played a part in leading to an infinitely more terrible war."[8]

THE EMPEROR IN EXILE

After his appeal to the League of Nations, Haile Selassie went into exile in Bath, England, where he remained for the next five years, occupying his time with the writing of an extensive history

of Ethiopia. Despite his depression, it is remarkable that throughout this period of intense suffering Haile Selassie was able to maintain his personal faith and courage as well as a humanitarian per-
spective.

As the tide turned in World War II, it became apparent that
the Italians were losing their foothold in Ethiopia. The Italian occupation there was fraught with difficulty. Not only was colonization an expensive liability yielding virtually nothing in return, but
the Italians also had to deal with marauding Ethiopian bandits
who attacked the foreign soldiers along the highways, railroad
tracks, and even in town, without warning. The geography of
Ethiopia made it difficult to effectively move troops and the
necessary supplies to maintain their European lifestyle. The
weather, too, was a factor. Under normal conditions in Ethiopia,
it rains solidly for four months out of the year, a very demoralizing
experience for those who are not accustomed to it. Coupled with
Italy's need to devote more energy to its fascist alliance with Germany, the Ethiopian occupation fell progressively lower on the
Italians' list of priorities.

Haile Selassie had been waiting for the right moment to make
his return to Ethiopia. On the advice of British intelligence the opportunity finally arrived. At the head of a joint British and
Sudanese (from the land of ancient Cush and Meroe) army, Haile
Selassie reentered Addis Ababa on May 5, 1941. The Italians, having retreated from the Allied powers into Eritrea, offered no
substantial resistance. Given a chance to exact his revenge, Haile
Selassie responded in the following manner:

> On this day which men on earth and angels in heaven
> could neither have foreseen nor known, I owe thanks
> unutterable by the mouth of man to the loving God who
> has enabled me to be present among you. Today is the
> beginning of a new era in the history of Ethiopia . . .
> Since this is so, do not reward evil for evil. Do not com-
> mit any act of cruelty like those which the enemy com-
> mitted against us up to this present time. Do not allow
> the enemy any occasion to foul the good name of
> Ethiopia. We shall take his weapons and make him
> return by the way he came.[9]

The remarkable compassion of this man is illuminated by

these words. His return to Ethiopia in 1941 as emperor undoubtedly qualifies him as *conquering lion*.

In spite of the Italians' rape of Ethiopia and the devastating loss of a generation of bright and creative men, there was a positive result of this tragedy in terms of African politics. Other Africans identified with Ethiopians as one of the oppressed peoples of Africa and recognized Ethiopia as "a country which they had at last learned to see as a solid island of freedom in the stormy waters of colonial oppression against which they were themselves struggling . . . "[10] The Italian conquest stimulated a feeling of unity among the blacks who came to regard the European aggression as an attack against the whole black race.

[1] Leonard O. Mosley, *The Conquering Lion*, p. 174.
[2] James Dugan, *Days of Emperor and Clown*, p. 172.
[3] Leonard O. Mosley, *The Conquering Lion*, p. 202.
[4] Peter Schwab, *Haile Selassie*, pp. 69-70.
[5] *Ibid.*, p. 71.
[6] *Ibid.*, p. 71.
[7] *Ibid.*, p. 71.
[8] *Ibid.*, p. 72.
[9] James Dugan, *Days of Emperor and Clown*, p. 352.
[10] S.K.B Asante, *Pan-African Protest: West Africa and the Italo-Ethiopian Crises, 1934-1941*, p. 17.

6

His Imperial Majesty

You must remember that Ethiopia is like a sleeping beauty, that time has stood still here for 2,000 years. We must take great care, therefore, not to overwhelm her with changes now that she is beginning to awaken from her long sleep.[1]

During his reign, Haile Selassie strived to accomplish in one lifetime what it took most European countries nearly a millennium to do. To aid Ethiopia in making the transition from a feudal and tribal society, loosely bound by a common greed for land, to a modern state that attempted to care for the physical and moral needs of its citizens was a goal of monumental proportions; and it is a tribute to the remarkable character of His Imperial Majesty that any progress was made at all. The obstacles in his path were numerous and solidly interwoven in the social fabric of Ethiopian life. Ironically, in the end, Haile Selassie was destroyed by those whose very lives he sought to uplift.

Haile Selassie inherited his zest for humanitarian reform from his predecessor Menelik II, as well as his father. As early as 1916, when he first consolidated his political power as regent, Ras Tafari began establishing hospitals, schools, and even a university in Addis Ababa to create a better standard of living and greater

61

opportunities for Ethiopians. Constantly distracted by the struggle to outwit his political enemies, he looked forward to a time when he could concentrate on extensive reform and modernization in his country.

It was not until many years after Haile Selassie first adjusted the crown on his head — almost immediately faced with the emergency of stalling the Italian invasion of Ethiopia, the subsequent war, defeat, and exile — that he was able to institute the land reforms that were so long overdue. It was during his peacetime reign, which lasted for more than thirty years, that His Imperial Majesty had the chance to realize his dreams for Ethiopia.

AN ERA OF PEACE

The image of the emperor was very much that of a father figure. The people of Ethiopia felt secure that he knew what was best for his country. When peace returned to Ethiopia, Haile Selassie immediately took steps to diffuse the three traditional conservative elements that threatened the centralized unity he wished to create. Thus, the church, the Ethiopian aristocracy, and the military all yielded to the magnetic and absolute power of the emperor.

In 1929, as Regent Ras Tafari, he had invested the first Ethiopian bishops, thus taking control of the Ethiopian Orthodox Church away from the Coptic Church of Alexandria in Egypt. In 1950, he appointed the first Ethiopian abuna, who answered directly to the emperor. By 1958, each of the fourteen provinces was appointed a bishop, and the abuna was elected from among and by this group of bishops. The structure of the church was completely rearranged in such a way that the emperor was not only the head of state, but Defender of the Faith as well. In this respect, he was the head of the Ethiopian church and served as a spiritual, as well as a political leader to his people.

In addition to this, as of 1942, the church was no longer exempt from paying taxes to the government, a significant levy since the church owned and leased over one-third of the land in Ethiopia. For years the church had been enjoying total tax exemption while exacting tributes, rents, and compensatory labor from its tenants.

Another significant result of this reorganization was the break-up of the church's monopoly on education for the Ethiopian people. For years it had exercised control of church schools, enabling only well-educated Ethiopians to become priests. In an ecumenical move, the emperor claimed that his citizens were to be Ethiopians first and Christians or Moslems second. In this way the ancient struggle between the Christians and Moslems in Ethiopia was officially neutralized. However, the chronic hostilities in the provinces of Eritrea along the Red Sea, Tigre, and the Ogaden bordering Somalia in the southeast, would prove an ongoing challenge to the emperor's abilities.

During his political apprenticeship in the court of Menelik II, and throughout his own rise to power, Haile Selassie realized that to preserve any centralized authority in Ethiopia the old nobility had to be dissolved. The rases had seen this coming, and many of them sided with the Italians in 1935 with the hope of holding on to their power. When Haile Selassie resumed power in 1941, his imperial army was considerably stronger than the regional armies of the rases, which had been virtually devastated and exhausted by the Italian occupation. Hence, the nobility lost its prestige as a military aristocracy. Meanwhile the emperor enhanced his power by establishing a new military elite, his personal Imperial Body Guard, which was created to keep even the Ethiopian army in check.

At the same time, the rases lost the right to collect federal taxes in their provinces, which in the past had gone straight into their pockets and had amassed huge fortunes for them. In 1942, the Ministry of Finance in Ethiopia instituted a uniform tax system similar to the Internal Revenue Service in the United States.

To make matters worse for the old lords, the emperor assigned to the Ministry of the Interior the task of redrawing provincial boundaries and appointing new governors to the new provinces. Although somewhat appeased by imperial grants of titles — seats in the Senate, diplomatic posts, and sometimes dynastic marriages into the royal family — without their traditional powers and prestige, the old nobility was humbled. Haile Selassie also made it a point to elevate bright, loyal, and humble native tribesmen (such as the Gallas) to positions of power in the government beside the aristocratic Amhara, thus creating a new elite.

One project in Ethiopian reform to which Haile Selassie paid particular attention was the creation of an educational standard for his country. He planned to have 80 percent of all Ethiopian school-age children enrolled in school by the 1980s. A primary motive for establishing an educated class in Ethiopian society was to enable intelligent, qualified people to fill important governmental positions. It was also intended to somehow fill the void left by the generation of creative and intelligent Ethiopians who were massacred during the Italian occupation. This void was perhaps the most significant factor in the huge chasm that was about to open up in Ethiopian society between the young and idealistic students — impatient for social change — and the emperor.

University students, white collar civil workers, labor leaders, some members of the military, and a handful of quick-tempered Eritrean separatists grew increasingly critical of the emperor's policies. Ethiopia became a land restless for change, and to understand what created such restlessness, one must look at the emperor himself. First of all, Haile Selassie's power was absolute. His status as emperor was regarded as divine, as is reflected in the Ethiopian Constitution of 1955: "By virtue of his Imperial Blood, as well as by the anointing he has received, the person of the Emperor is sacred. His dignity is inviolable and His power indisputable" (Articles 2 and 4). Because of this absolute authority, the emperor controlled the church, the army, parliament, the legal system — virtually every facet of Ethiopian life.

The emperor had the power to take land away and give it back for political reward. He had the power to initiate and approve legislation and to ratify international treaties. Since his leadership was unquestionable, no political parties were allowed in the country; there was no voice of opposition or criticism emanating from society at large, therefore a system of checks and balances was neither created nor proposed. Even labor unions did not gain the right to form until 1955.

Ethiopia enjoyed a period of tremendous stability, but — like young children who enjoy the security of their parents' home when too young to make their own decisions but then rebel when they see the shortcomings and limitations of the life by which they have been sheltered — it was only a matter of time before Ethiopian society began to demand more freedom.

Acceptance of this type of absolute rule was perhaps most difficult for the university students, whose horizons had been broadened by the knowledge of European and even other African countries' standards of living. They could not understand why social progress in Ethiopia was so slow. To add to their frustration, it was illegal for them to dissent; there was no political provision in the Ethiopian hierarchy to challenge the emperor.

The students — many of whom were tied to Ethiopia's past by long ancestral lines — failed to recognize the fact that Ethiopia had changed very little in 2,000 years and that uprooting such a traditional way of life too quickly and without a viable alternative with which to replace it would be a painful and costly endeavor. Like transplanting in a garden, such alterations required time for the roots to adjust to new soil and filter down to the substrata of Ethiopian society. Haile Selassie soon found himself caught between the vanguards of socialism, demanding land reform and taxation of the wealthy, and the landowners who refused to allow the government to even survey or assess their land. The peasants, content with the burdens they had borne since antiquity, were the slowest to change.

The military, too, was becoming more and more independent. The Ethiopian Army had the organization, the numbers (30,000 to 40,000 men), and the education to think for itself. Many officers received their training in the United States, whose substantial financial support equipped the army, the navy, and the air force. The first American military mission was established in Ethiopia in 1954, replacing the British, whose influence waned in 1951. The United States took over the British military communications base at Kagnew near Asmara, at an initial investment of $160 million. By 1973, Ethiopia had received over $210 million in military assistance from the United States,[2] who considered Ethiopia its strongest African ally. Additionally, the Israelis offered valuable skills in training battalion troops and commando police in anti-guerilla tactics geared, for the most part, toward battle at the Eritrean Liberation Front, and against the Somalian invaders in the Ogaden. Many other western European countries, including Sweden, also contributed to the Ethiopian military force.

The Ethiopian Army, which was originally created to counterbalance the regional armies of the rases, for the most part remained loyal to the emperor during the zenith of his power. However, the emperor's decision to create the Imperial Body Guard to check the power of the army would, in time, show a paradoxical twist of fate.

REVOLUTION

The most serious challenge to Haile Selassie's authority came in December 1960, while he was on a state visit to Brazil. In a clever but fanatical plot to sway the emperor's loyal followers and supporters, two conspirators attempted to use Crown Prince Asfa Woosen and Haile Selassie's trusted cousin Ras Imru to stage a coup d'état. On the evening of December 13, most of the Cabinet ministers and members of Parliament were urgently called to the palace, where they were subsequently held hostage. It was unclear whether the coup was supported by the army or the Imperial Body Guard, who surrounded the army's checkpoints in Addis Ababa. Amidst this confusion, each arm of the military accused the other and revolution was in the air.

On the following day, the crown prince read a speech (which was most likely prepared for him) over the radio and declared that the old regime had come to an end. He stated that he would attempt to liberate the people of Ethiopia who "have lived by words and promises which have never been fulfilled." The broadcast later claimed that the coup was supported by the army, the police, and the young educated class. The students released a statement over the air proclaiming, "The new government is doing all in its power to free you from all oppression, giving you freedom of speech, press, and political parties."[3]

By December 16, the emperor had returned from Brazil after hearing news of the revolt. Meanwhile, the army and the Imperial Body Guard were engaged in intense fighting. After three days, the revolt was overpowered and the monarchy preserved intact. In a final act of desperation, the rebels assassinated fifteen of the twenty-one high level Ethiopian officials who had been held hostage, a merciless act that struck a harsh blow to the emperor.

Investigation revealed that the two main conspirators were brothers, Mengistu and Girmame Neway. This discovery was most painful to the emperor because Mengistu had served in the Imperial Body Guard for fifteen years, first as a deputy commander and then as a commander. His brother Girmame had been governor of a subprovince in Sidamo. The emperor's cousin, a governor in Tigre, had also figured in the plot. Among the conspirators were the commissioner of police and the chief of security, and other members of the elite Moja clan of Shoa (Shoa is the home province of Addis Ababa, Ethiopia's capital).

Perhaps Mengistu's loyalty, once firm and unquestionable, changed when he was rejected as a suitor to one of the emperor's granddaughters. It seems, however, that the real impetus for the plot to overthrow the emperor came from his brother Girmame, who had once been a graduate student at Columbia University in the United States. As a governor in Ethiopia, he had a reputation for progressiveness and outspoken hostility toward the nobility and foreign missionaries. He was also known to have an extensive library on the principles of Marxism. Although he enjoyed antagonizing the conservative element, Girmame also seemed to have genuine humanitarian goals. However, after being demoted by the conservatives, Girmame grew resentful and began to organize ideas of revolution with his brother's friends.

The month before the coup, the chief of security discovered the plot and chose to join the conspirators out of his admiration for Mengistu Neway. The chief of police did not join the group until the attempted coup was underway.

Students were brought into the fold by a number of officers of the Imperial Body Guard (including Girmame) who were taking courses at the University College of Addis Ababa. During courses on constitutional history, European history, and economics, there was a great deal of open and opinionated discussion, out of which grew an acute awareness of Ethiopia's backwardness. Although the students did not play a physical role in the rebellion, they supported its principles in essence.

Among the six hostages who survived assassination were the crown prince, the highly esteemed Ras Imru, and the emperor's son-in-law, Ras Massai. In a press conference after the coup, Emperor Haile Selassie explained, "The force which motivated these men was clearly personal ambition and lust for power," an analysis which was perhaps oversimplified. Later, reflecting on his own intentions gone awry, the emperor observed somewhat prophetically, "Trees that are planted do not always bear the desired fruit."[4]

In January 1961, Girmame was shot and killed while resisting capture. His brother Mengistu survived long enough to stand trial before he was executed. Before he died, he prophesied that the forces that gave rise to the coup, although thwarted for the moment, would eventually achieve ultimate success.

To appease the spirit of rebellion, Haile Selassie appointed younger members to the Cabinet and gave the army a raise in salary (at the expense of the civil servants, who received an equal pay cut). The emperor also lessened his dependence on the army by establishing a territorial militia. The crown prince and Ras Imru were excused of any unintentional misconduct and restored to their positions in the royal hierarchy. After the 1960 coup, many reforms were made as concessions to those who would otherwise give rise to challenge. Land and tax reforms, although difficult to institute at the grass-roots level, were proposed in 1966 and 1967. The Senate voted down the land reform bill in 1966 but the Chamber of Deputies successfully reduced the landowners' percentage of growers' crops, and tenant farmers were freed of other obligations to their tyrannical landlords. However, the old aristocracy resisted the new tax law of 1967 by refusing to allow the survey and assessment of their lands.

HAILE SELASSIE AS A WORLD LEADER

In spite of Ethiopia's simmering internal affairs after the attempted coup, most of the world regarded Haile Selassie's power as solid, exemplified by his ability to put down the revolt within three days. The emperor further elevated his prestige as a world leader by hosting the conference of the African Heads of State in Addis Ababa in 1963.

By virtue of his sophistication and experience in international affairs, Haile Selassie was greatly admired by many African leaders, including Jomo Kenyatta, the President of Kenya, and Kwame Nkrumah of Ghana, the founder of modern *pan-Africanism*. Pan-African consciousness is defined as "the consciousness of belonging to the African continent and the Negro race, the awareness of membership in that distinctive race, and the desire to maintain the integrity and assert the equality of that race."[5]

By the same token, Ethiopia had become a symbol for Africa's struggle for independence from European colonialism. It was regarded by the rest of the oppressed African states as "the shrine enclosing the last sacred spark of African political freedom, the impregnable rock of African resistance against white invasion, a living symbol, an incarnation of African independence."[6]

Since antiquity, Ethiopia has borne great meaning for the black people as a whole, referring not only to a race of dark-skinned people but also to the existence of the ancient African civilization of Cush, and later, Egypt. The words of Psalm 68 in the Bible have been regarded as prophecy, as a kind of birthright of Ethiopians (and in a larger sense Africans) as a chosen race: "He hath scattered the peoples who delight in war; princes shall come

out of Egypt; Ethiopia shall stretch out her hands unto God"
(Psalm 68:31). This promise ignited the torch of liberation for a
united pan-African state in the continent of Africa and kindled the
flames of the back-to-Africa movement of repatriation in the
United States. This will be discussed in greater depth in the following chapter, but it is helpful to understand in what high regard
Haile Selassie was held, even while he was alive. The existence of
an African Christian king, descended through the Solomonic line,
was for Africa a dream come true, a fulfillment of prophecy.[7]

For this reason it is not surprising that Addis Ababa became
the capital for pan-African unity and the headquarters for the
Organization of African States. In 1958, Ethiopia attended the
first conference on Independent African States in Ghana,
represented by the emperor's son, Prince Sahle Selassie. At first,
the Ethiopian delegation was sensitive to the criticism of its absolute monarch in a time when other African states were striving
for democracy, but overall response to the Ethiopians was warm
and fraternal. In 1958 the emperor also proposed the establishment of the African Development Bank, to encourage African
economic independence. The bank eventually opened in 1963.
Also in the early 1960s, the United Nations created the United Nations Economic Commission for Africa in Addis Ababa. The commission served to support refugees from other oppressed African
nations, such as South Africa. Politically, the Ethiopian delegation to the United Nations openly condemned the South African
policy of apartheid (living apart or segregation of races) and supported the limitation of French nuclear testing in the Sahara.

In late 1962, Haile Selassie extended invitations to all African
leaders, from Abdul Nassar of Egypt to Nkrumah of Ghana, to
participate in a joint conference of African unity to be held in May
1963 in Addis Ababa. The conference was an overwhelming success, and as a result Haile Selassie was appointed president of the
newly founded Organization of African Unity, centered in Addis
Ababa. Ethiopia effectively became the voice for Africa in the
arena of world affairs, in the United Nations, and in diplomatic
relations with world powers such as the United States. The radical
tone of pan-African policy was somewhat altered by Haile Selassie
into a more sophisticated and realistic direction. On a more
physical level, the nations of Africa were now united by a joint
African bank and by extended air connections as a result of Ethiopian Air Lines.

As an African leader, Haile Selassie had numerous opportunities to call upon his diplomatic skills, intervening in the Moroccan-Algerian border dispute of 1963, attempting to reconcile the differences between Ghana and Guinea after the fall of Nkrumah, and mediating in the Nigerian-Biafra disputes that had occurred since 1968. Under pressure from the Ethiopian delegation, the United Nations adopted a resolution in June 1968, proclaiming that southwest Africa be known as Namibia and forcing South Africa's withdrawal from that territory.[8] More noteworthy than Haile Selassie's influence in the political forefront was the invitation of brotherhood that he extended to twenty million black Americans of African descent, praising them in their struggle for freedom and urging them to lend their talents and skills in support of Africa's struggle for dignity and progress.[9]

FALL OF THE EMPEROR

In the face of Haile Selassie's many great accomplishments at both the national and international level, it is difficult to understand how such a seemingly invincible man could fall from power. Cursed and degraded by his people, rather than being allowed to die gracefully and in peace, the political demise of Haile Selassie is a painful story to tell.

The blame for Haile Selassie's fall from power rests with no one individual or group of people. The only person at which a finger can really be pointed is the aging emperor himself, who was slowly losing control over his empire and even his own life. He should have relinquished the throne years earlier, but had chosen not to do so, possibly because his only surviving son was implicated in the plot to overthrow him in 1960. With the death of his two daughters, his wife, Menen, and his favorite son, Prince Sahle Selassie, who was killed in an automobile accident in 1957, Haile Selassie had lost all that was dear to him.

The emperor became a victim of circumstance. The simple fact that Haile Selassie was in his late seventies during the worldwide student riots of 1967, 1968, and 1969 — which affected Ethiopia as deeply as they affected the United States — is of great significance. Exhausted by the tremendous burden of more than fifty years of responsibility as a statesman, the emperor retreated into his own world within the palace, increasingly leaving decision-making powers in the hands of Prime Minister Habte Wold. The

Parliament and the Council of Ministers provided little support because they were still comprised mainly of the old Amharic aristocracy whose interests were more self-serving than patriotic.

As a result, funds were mismanaged and economic growth was reduced to a pitiful 2 percent annual rate. Only 5 percent of the lands at imperial disposal were distributed among the poor. Education projects came to a standstill, and land and tax reforms were in a a stalemate.

The emperor, of course, took the blame for his government's ineffectiveness. Perhaps rightly so, but the people of Ethiopia may have been shortsighted in their cooperation with the social changes Haile Selassie proposed. The result was a compromise that truly satisfied no one.

The drought and famine that began in 1972 and continues into the present, parching the whole of Ethiopia and draining its very lifeblood, was the most devastating event leading specifically to the downfall of Haile Selassie. It actually began in 1970, a year when only light rains fell following nearly a decade of unpredictable rainfall, alternating between drought and deluge. The harvest at the end of 1971 was poor, and very little surplus grain was sent to the imperial storehouse. Peasants began to eat their reserves of planting seeds, hoping for improvement that did not come. 1972 was another bad year, with crop yields ranging from below average to total loss. Many provinces went without seed that year. By 1973 there was nothing to harvest and no seed to plant, which would have made little difference in light of the fact that there was no rain.

Finally, in late 1973, the rain came in a torrent. Instead of providing relief, it destroyed crops and washed away precious topsoil. In many ways, the drought and famine were results of centuries of poor crop rotation, soil erosion, and extensive destruction of natural forests (for firewood), which left only 3 percent of the land still wooded. By this time, work animals having had little water to drink and no grass to graze began dying. Out of starvation, many of Ethiopia's poor peasants and farmers ate their animals, and as a result there were few left to use for planting and harvesting crops.

The situation worsened as famine and disease spread to epidemic proportions. Tens of thousands of people were dying and hundreds of thousands were sick and starving. Cholera invaded the refugee camps, killing men, women, and children without mercy. The following description gives a vivid picture of the suffering: "In the spring, tens of thousands of people — first the men, then the women and children, then a few elderly — began straggling into the market towns along the Addis-Asmara highway. By May 1973, travelers saw them resting beneath lean-tos along the roadside. Some died on the highway. Others flagged the vehicles to beg for food. Truckers started complaining that they couldn't get through, and some hauled bags of bread and tossed them as they sped by."[10]

The greatest crime toward the Ethiopian people was the government's unwillingness to help them. With characteristic Ethiopian pride, the Imperial government sought to solve its own problems, refusing foreign aid from world relief organizations. Because aid generally had to be requested, or prefaced by a statement describing the condition of the emergency, nothing was done. Journalists and the world news media caught wind of the story and accused the Ethiopian government of an intentional cover-up, first on its own behalf and second, from the various United Nations–related agencies that were trying to help. Shockingly enough, the United Nations agencies, desiring to preserve working relations with the emperor, actually complied with these requests of silence from the Ethiopian government. It wasn't until foreign journalists smuggled out newspaper and film reports of the mass starvation occurring in Ethiopia, in the provinces of Wollo and Tigre, and later in the south (Sidamo and Harar), that any international attention was brought into focus. International outcry put pressure on the Ethiopian government to accept relief and cease the unnecessary suffering of its people.

Eventually the aid did come, but too late for the nearly one million people who died of starvation between 1973 and 1975. Tragically, the foreign food and grain delivered to the docks of Asmara and Djibouti didn't always reach the intended destinations. Railway and truckers' strikes paralyzed transportation, and much of the food rotted while Ethiopians in the interior starved to death. There were also those who re-bagged the donated grain and sold it on the open market at a hefty profit. Corruption in times like these — especially when a waning central authority was blind to such injustices — was inevitable.

Undeniably, when the emperor blatantly ignored the drought crisis and resulting starvation, he proved himself incapable of effectively ruling his country. His unrealistic evaluation of the situation cost him everything. So, when the military gave birth to a Soviet-influenced body called the *Derg*, Haile Selassie bowed and agreed to a constitutional monarchy. The resignation of Prime Minister Habte Wold was also demanded, and conceded, and Endalkachew Makonnen was sworn in on February 28, 1974, with the purpose of creating a new Cabinet. Concession after concession was granted, and soon the emperor witnessed the arrests of many of his top officials. The *creeping coup* had begun.

On July 22, 1974, Endalkachew Makonnen was arrested. He resigned and was replaced by the old and beloved imperial ally, Ras Imru. However, labor strikes, student demonstrations, and mounting pressure made the military aware that a total change in the current structure of government was necessary.

On September 12, 1974, the Provisional Military Administration Council (PMAC) presented His Imperial Majesty Haile Selassie I with the following proclamation:

Haile Selassie I, who has ruled the country ever since he assumed power as a crown prince, has abused the authority, dignity, and honor of office for the personal benefit and interest of himself, his immediate family, and his retainers.[11]

A later statement further specified:

The Wollo tragedy is a crime against the Ethiopian people for the simple reason that relief-aid was deliberately denied a starving population. Haile Selassie's self-serving regime chose to protect the image of the head of state rather than to save the lives of the starving masses. The discredited government chose to condemn hundreds of thousands of people to slow, agonizing death for the glorification of one man.[12]

Haile Selassie's response to these and other accusations was characteristically dignified and accepting. Witnessed by a trusted friend, Haile Selassie's dethronement was described as follows:

The emperor agreed to the terms of the proclamation and said, according to the committee's statement, that if the committee was deposing him for the good of the country,

then he did not oppose them. Changes, he said, occurred
all over the world from time to time and, as this change
was for the benefit of the Ethiopian people, he welcomed
it.[13]

In spite of the senility of his later years, Haile Selassie's
underlying love for his people and his country is apparent, and the
words of the PMAC must have bitterly stung the aged emperor.
On September 12, 1974, the emperor was arrested, the constitution
suspended, the Parliament, the Crown Council, and the Imperial
Court dissolved. Over 2,000 years of monarchy had come to an
end.

The emperor disappeared, and some say he was hospitalized
after an extensive fast. Whatever the case may be, he left his
palace, humiliated and brokenhearted.

What took place in Ethiopia in the following months was
nothing short of chaos. General Aman, who took power after
September 12, 1974, was assassinated along with sixty others (including the two ex-prime ministers) for being sympathetic to
Eritrean separatists. November 23, 1974, was called Bloody Saturday. The crown prince, who originally was to have inherited the title of king and ruled as a constitutional monarch, was never invited to return to Ethiopia. Major Mengistu Haile Mariam[14]
emerged as the strongman of the PMAC, and introduced a
definitely pro-Marxist/Leninist political doctrine that was officially adopted in 1977. He opened Ethiopia's doors to massive Soviet
aid and allowed Cuban troops to help police any opposition.
When it joined the Liberation Parties in Eritrea, Tigre, Sidamo,
Somali, Afar, and other states in 1975, the newly formed Ethiopian People's Revolutionary Party (EPRP) called for a civilian
government. When the patriarch of the Ethiopian Orthodox
Church, Abuna Tewofloes, was deposed in February 1976, the
Ethiopian people were robbed of their religious guidance. The
country was in the throes of civil war. In the power struggle that
ensued, friend was pitted against friend, executions were commonplace, and a dark cloud of oppression settled over the country.

Haile Selassie quietly died in August 1975, in an unknown
place of an unknown cause. Little was revealed by the PMAC. To
those who remember him in a positive light, His Imperial Majesty's
life and actions are an inspiration and a hope for the liberation of

Ethiopia and the entire black race. To those who choose to cast a dark shadow on his life, the appalling loss of life in the devastating drought and ensuing famine made Ras Tafari guilty of second-degree genocide, a step away from Hitler. It is up to the world to decide whether he was truly a monster or a Messiah.

[1] Robert L. Hess, *Ethiopia*, p. 106.
[2] Irving Kaplan, ed., *Ethiopia: A Country Study*, p. 45.
[3] Robert L. Hess, *Ethiopia*, p. 135.
[4] Robert L. Hess, *Ethiopia*, p. 141.
[5] S. K. B. Asante, *Pan*-African Protest, pp. 9-11.
[6] Daniel Thwaite, *The Seething African Pot*, p. 207.
[7] S. K. B. Asante, *Pan-African Protest*, pp. 9-11.
[8] *London Times*, p. 8.
[9] *Ebony*, pp. 29-32.
[10] Jack Shepherd, *Politics of Starvation*, p. 19.
[11] *Bulletin of the African Institute*, Issue #7, 1975, p. 243.
[12] PMAC Ministry of Information, 1975.
[13] "Constitutional Developments in Ethiopia," *Africa Research Bulletin* (Sept. 1-30, 1974), p. 3360.
[14] An uncanny similarity to the man behind the 1960 coup.

7

The Rastafarians

THE FIRST WAVE

While Haile Selassie was still alive, a movement was born in Jamaica, glorifying him as God. Even though His Majesty agreed that his position as the emperor of Ethiopia was divinely sanctioned, he was somewhat surprised by the news that the Rastafarians of Jamaica regarded him as the black man's Messiah. In the 1920s, before Ras Tafari was crowned emperor, Marcus Garvey made a cryptic prophecy to the displaced black Africans of the Western world. In a church in Kingston, Jamaica, in 1927, Garvey prophesied, "Look to Africa, where a black king shall be crowned, for the day of deliverance is here." Haile Selassie was crowned emperor in 1930; thus was born the messianic movement of the Rastafarians. Haile Selassie is their God, born in the flesh for the redemption of the entire black race.

Marcus Garvey's words made a deep impression on his black listeners who, after centuries of oppression at the hands of the white race, no longer wanted to worship a white man's God. According to the Rastafarians, the doctrines of Christianity were adapted to suit the ambitions of white imperialism, and were no longer adequate to fulfill the spiritual needs of the black race. In Jamaica, black Christian ministers were regarded with contempt and disgust by the Rastafarians, who viewed them as puppets of the white ruling class and traitors to their own race. The irony of this is that Haile Selassie himself was a devout Christian, a staunch member of the Ethiopian Orthodox Church, and spiritual figurehead in his own country.

The Rastafarians rely on an assortment of quotations from the Bible to endorse their beliefs. These quotations, sometimes taken loosely and out of context, are interpreted freely to prove that blacks are destined to be the ultimate rulers of the world. From their interpretation of Jeremiah 8:21, the Rastafarians are convinced that God is black: "For the hurt of the daughter of my people am I hurt; I am black; astonishment hath taken hold of me." In Daniel 7:9, the last king of kings is described this way: "And I beheld till the thrones were cast down and the Ancient of Days did sit, whose garment was white as snow, and the hair of his head like pure wool; his throne was like the fiery flame, and his wheels as burning fire." Simon of Cyrene, who bore the cross for Christ at his crucifixion, was allegedly an African. Psalm 87:3 makes reference to the fact that the redeemer was to come out of Ethiopia: "Glorious things are spoken of thee, O city of God Selah. I will make mention of Rehab and Babylon to them that know me: Behold Philistia, and Tyre, with Ethiopia; this man was born there." Even a group of Christian missionaries visiting Ethiopia in 1930 mentioned, "The present Emperor is the great hope of Ethiopia . . . The prophecy does not assure us that Ethiopia shall stretch forth her hands to Western civilization, but to God."[1]

Shortly after Marcus Garvey's prophecy, the four founding fathers of the Rastafarian movement, Archibald Dunkley, Leonard Howell, Joseph Hibbert, and Robert Hinds, consolidated their beliefs and their leadership. Archibald Dunkley spent two years studying the scriptures in order to determine whether Haile Selassie was indeed the black king of whom Garvey had spoken. After reading Ezekiel 30, I Timothy 6, Revelation 17 and 19, and Isaiah 43, Dunkley agreed that His Majesty was the Messiah and opened a mission in Kingston, in 1933, where he preached "Ras Tafari" as God, as the king of kings, and as the root of David. All four founders were ministers whose followers believed, as they did, in the divinity of Haile Selassie. In time, Leonard Howell emerged as the strongest of the four fathers, and with Robert Hinds as his deputy, he continued to preach from his well-established ministry in Kingston.

This early phase of the Rastafarian movement can be labeled *the first wave*, which was characterized by zealous idealism, unrealistic expectations, and hostility toward the established political order in Jamaica. Many believed that Haile Selassie would literally come to their rescue and break the chains of their oppression. The early Rastafarians frequently found themselves in jail as a result of their antagonizing rhetoric and outlandish schemes for fund raising. At one point, Howell organized his followers to sell 5,000 photographs of Haile Selassie, at a shilling each, as passports to Ethiopia. At the site of the Morant Bay Rebellion of 1865 (one hundred years earlier), Howell and Hinds were arrested, tried, and sentenced. Later they were joined by Dunkley and Hibbert. The first wave of Rastafarians made the mistake of becoming too easily embroiled in the politics of the island. They fought the white oppressors — especially the police — on their own terms, overtly challenging Jamaican society and giving the Rastafarian movement a dangerous and violent reputation. This undercurrent of lawlessness was not transcended until the late 1960s when reggae music became the prime medium for the movement's ideology. The music, which seems to invite rather than provoke, introduced a more sophisticated (and legal) channel for delivering the Rastafarian message to the world.

MARCUS GARVEY

Before a true evaluation of the Rastafarians can be made, it is necessary to understand how Marcus Garvey succeeded in awakening black consciousness. Born in Jamaica in 1887, Marcus Mosiah Garvey was descended from the Maroon tribes, a longtime radical element involved with local black independence that initiated the Morant Bay Rebellion of 1865. At the age of fifteen, Garvey became involved with radical journalism and promoted the *back to Africa* movement, otherwise known as repatriation.

In 1916 Marcus Garvey went to the United States, originally to meet with Booker T. Washington, his ideological mentor. Although Washington died before Garvey had the opportunity to meet him, the young radical continued to strive for black organization. He made his way to Harlem and once there founded the Universal Negro Improvement Association, which became the means through which he sought to realize his ideological dreams. His success was phenomenal, and within a few years, the UNIA

LOS GATOS H.S. LIBRARY

Marcus Garvey, leader of the "Back to Africa" movement

claimed a membership of two million in the United States. Garvey also started his own newspaper, *Negro World*, whose rallying cry was, "One Aim, One God, One Destiny." During the next two years, Marcus Garvey popularized his UNIA movement by opening offices across the United States and addressing crowds wherever he went.

Hailed as a black savior and prophet, Marcus Garvey's words stirred his listeners: "The time has come for those of us who have the vision of the future to inspire our people to a closer kinship, to a closer love of self, because only through this appreciation of self will we be able to rise to that higher life that will make us not an extinct race in the future, but a race of men fit to survive."[2] He rallied crowds by stating, "I am not opposed to the white race, as charged by my enemies. I have no time to hate anyone. All my time is devoted to the upbuilding and development of the Negro race."[3] "The world ought to know that it can't keep 400 million Negroes down forever."[4] Marcus Garvey further specified his intentions: "The political readjustment of the world means this — that every race must find a home; hence the great cry of Palestine for the Jews — Ireland for the Irish — India for the Indians and simultaneously . . . Africa for the Africans."[5] "I pray God [sic] that we shall never use our physical prowess to oppress the human race, but we will use our strength, physically, morally, and otherwise to preserve humanity and civilization."[6]

Reflecting upon black history, Marcus Garvey said, "Be as proud of your race today as our fathers were in days of yore. We have a beautiful history, and we shall create another in the future that will astonish the world."[7] He went on to say, "But when we come to consider the history of men, was not the Negro a power, was he not great once? Yet, honest students of history can recall the day when Egypt, Ethiopia, and Timbuctu towered in their civilization, towered over Europe, towered above Asia. When Europe was inhabited by a race of cannibals, a race of savages, naked men, heathens and pagans, Africa was peopled with a race of black men, who were cultured and refined, men who, it is said, were like the gods."[8]   It is precisely the history recounted in the early chapters of this book to which Marcus Garvey was referring.

Marcus Garvey's doctrine was not one of hatred for the whites, but rather of elevation and equality for the black race. Denouncing mob violence, Marcus Garvey said, "Violence and injustice have never helped a race or nation . . . we as a people in this new age desire to love all mankind . . . in keeping with the Divine Injunction, 'Man, love thy brother.'"[9] In this respect Marcus Garvey's words parallel those of Haile Selassie, who also did not advocate violence and who chose to forgive his enemies.

This positive vibration was the foundation for the second wave of the Rastafarian movement, whose members believed in a new world order to be established by blacks, part of which required physical repatriation to Africa.

In 1919, Marcus Garvey founded a steamship company called the Black Star Line, with the purpose of commercially linking blacks all over the world. Stock was sold at five dollars a share and was available only to blacks. In 1920, the Black Star Line began trading between New York and Jamaica on its freighter the *SS Frederick Douglass*. It was also promised that the Black Star Line would begin the physical process of transporting blacks back to Africa.

What was needed was a place to begin an African colony. In the early 1920s, Marcus Garvey began conducting intense negotiations with the Liberian government to establish colonies in Liberia with UNIA members, where black emigrants from the West would be received. Liberia was founded in 1822 as a result of the successful colonization in Sierra Leone of *free* (preemancipation) blacks from Britain and the United States. This tentative plan with Liberia promised to be the climax of Marcus Garvey's UNIA movement. Then, mysteriously, on the eve of the first shipment of UNIA advisors and supplies in 1924, Liberian President King changed his mind. It is suspected that President King bowed to pressure from the United States government, acting on behalf of the Firestone Rubber Company which subsequently leased a million acres of Liberian land for rubber plantations. Marcus Garvey also suspected that his arch rival, W.E.B. DuBois, played a hand in this sudden betrayal. DuBois, an American black political leader of Garvey's time, was opposed to the concept of repatriation and what he considered Garvey's radical politics. It is possible that DuBois persuaded President King that Garvey was a dangerous man.

Liberia's change of plans ruined those of Marcus Garvey. His promise to take blacks back to Africa was now an empty one, and on this basis, the United States government proceeded with charges of mail fraud and tax evasion as a result of the money he had elicited from blacks expecting to return to Africa. With no records to prove his case, Marcus Garvey was convicted and jailed in 1925.

President Calvin Coolidge commuted the sentence in 1927 in exchange for the political support given to him by the UNIA during his election, and Marcus Garvey was allowed to return to Jamaica. Although he had been publicly humiliated and his spirit broken, Garvey's belief in the black cause never waned. Abandoned by his followers, he later moved to England where he died of pneumonia in 1940. Ironically, Marcus once prophesied that leadership ends in pain and death.

Nevertheless, the repercussions of Marcus Garvey's message continue to carry waves of enlightenment to black people throughout the world. "No other black man in history was able to understand so clearly the worldwide oppressions of black people, and no other was in turn perceived by so many blacks as the one person with solutions to their problems."[10] Marcus Garvey's influence was felt from Jomo Kenyatta of Kenya to Kwame Nkrumah of Ghana. His words made a profound impression on Malcolm X, the United States leader of the Black Muslims, who praised Marcus Garvey by saying, "All the freedom movement that is taking place right here in America today was initiated by the philosophy and teachings of Garvey. The entire black nationalist philosophy here in America is fed upon the seeds that were planted by Marcus Garvey."[11] Even Martin Luther King saluted him, saying, "Marcus Garvey was the first man of color in the history of the United States to lead and develop a mass movement . . . to give millions of Negroes a sense of dignity and destiny, and make the Negro feel he was somebody."[12]

By 1952, Marcus Garvey was proclaimed a national hero in Jamaica, and since that time, Rastafarians have revered Marcus Garvey as the man who inspired their movement. "His speeches are avidly read, songs and poems are written in his honor, and in the pantheon of Rastafarians, Marcus Garvey is second only to Haile Selassie."[13]

The following words belong to the *Ethiopian Song*, which was first used by Marcus Garvey as the UNIA anthem and later adopted as the national song of the Rastafarians:

> *Ethiopia thou land of our Fathers*
> *Thou land where the gods love to be*
> *As storm clouds at night sudden*
> *Our armies come rushing to thee.*
> *With the Red, Gold, and Green floating o'er us*
> *And the emperor to shield us from wrong.*

With a God and a future before us
We hail and we shout with this song.

Chorus:

Long live our Negus, Negus I.
And keep Ethiopia free to advance
To advance with truth and right,
To advance with truth and light,
With righteous leading we hasten to our
God and KING humanity pleading one
God for us all.[14]

THE SECOND WAVE

The political doctrine of the second wave of the Rastafarian movement had six basic tenets: First, they believed Haile Selassie to be the living God. Second, there existed the belief that blacks are the reincarnation of the ancient Israelites who, at the hand of the white people, have been exiled in Jamaica. Third, there was the implication that whites are inferior to blacks. Fourth, the Jamaican political situation was viewed as a hopeless issue, and life in Ethiopia was considered salvation. Fifth, the invincible emperor of Ethiopia was personally arranging for expatriated persons of African origin to return to Ethiopia. And finally, many believed – and many still believe – that in the near future blacks will rule the world after Babylon destroys itself through a nuclear holocaust.[15] (Babylon is the Rastafarian's metaphor used to describe the Western capitalist system, which the Rastas believe thrives on greed, corruption, and exploitation. In their eyes, by its very nature Babylon is doomed to self-destruction.)

This second wave of Rastafarians believed in the imminent repatriation of blacks to Africa. Fed by the prophesies of Marcus Garvey, many oriented their entire lives to this forthcoming event. The fact that these people believed in their deliverance so literally, expressed the hopelessness of their lives in Jamaica, their desire to escape it, and their willingness to focus on a potential deliverer.

After he was released from jail, Leonard Howell, one of the more radical early Rasta leaders, retreated into the mountains of Jamaica and in 1940 started the Pinnacle community. Established by his organization, the Ethiopian Salvation Society, the commune at Pinnacle became and continues to be the prototype for Rastafarian living. Because Rastafarians choose not to be part of the real estate system of Babylon and, instead, *capture* their lands from the government, they are essentially considered squatters. Initially the entrance to the commune was secret, only known to the Rasta brethren, and was heavily guarded by dogs.

In the 1940s and early 1950s, the community, which ranged in population from 500 to 1,600 members, was supported through the cultivation and sale of Jamaica's largest cash crop, ganja (otherwise known as marijuana). Ganja had been outlawed in the early 1920s by the British authorities under the Dangerous Drug Law, which subsequently classified the Rastafarians as outlaws living beyond the fringes of Jamaican society. This brought them into repeated conflicts with the police, who, without warning, raided and imprisoned cult members on a regular basis. Howell's ability to evade the police brought further glory to the leader.

When the Jamaican police broke up the Pinnacle community in 1954, most of the Rastafarians moved to the slums of the *Back o'the Wall*, a shantytown in Kingston, to await the sign of a better life. In 1955, the hope for repatriation was rekindled when Haile Selassie donated 500 acres of Ethiopian land to members of the Ethiopian World Federation (a Rastafarian organization based in New York City), who had helped him in his war effort against Italy.

By invitation of the eminent Ras Emanuel of Jamaica, the Reverend Claudius Henry visited the 1958 Grounation (a Rastafarian ceremony of spiritual communion, involving drumming, chanting, and the smoking of ganja). A year later, Reverend Henry exploited the islanders' desire for a deliverer, calling himself a modern-day Moses and saying he would lead them back to the Promised Land. He endeavored to accomplish this feat by selling repatriation cards for one shilling apiece. The card read, "Pioneering Israel's scattered children of African origin 'Back home to Africa.' This year, 1959, deadline date October 5th: This new government is God's righteous kingdom of peace on Earth. 'Creation's second birth' . . . Please reserve this certificate for removal. No passport will be necessary for those returning to Africa . . . "[15]

On the appointed day, October 5, 1959, thousands of Rastafarians flocked to the address given on the card. Many had sold their homes, land, and all material possessions in anticipation of their return to Africa. Without the necessary passports, book-ings, or reservations, not to mention ships, planes, or money, all Reverend Henry could do was stand before the crowd empty-handed. The organizer awkwardly explained that the specified date was intended as a deadline for the Jamaican government to make arrangements with His Majesty for the exportation of Jamaicans. Needless to say, the explanation was lost on Reverend Henry's crowd, who had given up everything for a hollow promise.[16]

This fiasco was characteristic of the beliefs of the second wave of Rastafarians who were perhaps less violent than the first wave, but more desperate and naive in their expectations. In 1960, a United Nations representative from Ghana spoke at a library in Kingston, advising the Rastafarians that no African country would accept unskilled laborers from Jamaica, especially if they were un-willing to work as well. He went on to say that "a destitute and un-skilled migrant would have to be in a position to trace his ancestors and to have these ancestors support him . . . " He encouraged them to find Africa within themselves, declaring, "Africa is everywhere, Jamaica is Africa!"[17] Not surprisingly, the Rasta-farians were not impressed and left in disagreement.

THE THIRD WAVE

It wasn't until Haile Selassie's state visit to Jamaica on April 21, 1966, that the myth of physical repatriation to Ethiopia was dispelled by the emperor himself. The emperor's arrival in Jamaica was heralded by the Rastafarians as a divine occasion. Haile Selassie's jet flew in from the east out of the dawn, and when the Imperial Lion was seen on the fuselage, thousands of Dreads (Rastafarians who wear their hair in long, matted dreadlocks) broke through police lines and ran to the plane. Hundreds crouched in the shade cast by the Imperial Lion's wings and lit their chalices (huge, flamboyant goat's horn water-pipes used for smoking ganja). Haile Selassie walked through the door, stood at the top of the ramp, and beheld ten thousand Dreads crushed around his plane, smoking, chanting, praising his name, and fall-ing on their foreheads. He took one long look, turned around, stepped back into his plane, and had the door shut. For another hour, the emperor refused to come out.[18]

Later during the three-day festivities, several Rasta brethren were invited to a cocktail party held for the emperor at the prestigious King's House, a governmental residence. It is reported that a private communication between the emperor and the Rastafarians took place at that time, during which Haile Selassie told them that the brethren should not seek immigration to Ethiopia until they succeeded in liberating the people of Jamaica. The new ideology, *liberation before migration*, was created as a result of this meeting.

This new outlook — having come from the lips of the emperor himself — gave rise to the third wave of the Rastafarian movement. Messages from this third wave have been popularized through the reggae music of Bob Marley, Peter Tosh, and many others. These musical prophets started a wave of Rastafarian music so powerful that its crest is still breaking around the world. Added to the new prestige of the Rastafarian movement in Jamaica, resulting from His Imperial Majesty's visit and its acceptance in principle by the new socialist government of Michael Manley, it is altogether possible that the Rastafarians might someday realize their dreams of a true home for the black man under the guidance of Jah.

[1] Stuart Bergsma, *Rainbow Empire*, p. 110.

[2] Amy Jacques-Garvey, ed., *Philosophy and Opinions of Marcus Garvey*, p. 64.

[3] *Ibid.*, p. 13.

[4] *Ibid.*, p. 9.

[5] *Ibid.*, p. 34.

[6] *Ibid.*, p. 11.

[7] *Ibid.*, p. 7.

[8] *Ibid.*, p. 57.

[9] *Ibid.*, p. 12.

[10] Leonard E. Barrett, *The Rastafarians: Sounds of Cultural Dissonance*, p. 66.

[11] Leonard E. Barrett, *The Rastafarians: A Study in Messianic Cultism in Jamaica*, p. 62.

[12] *Ibid.*, p. 62.

[13] Leonard E. Barrett, *The Rastafarians: Sounds of Cultural Dissonance*, p. 67.

[14] Leonard E. Barrett, *The Rastafarians: A Study in Messianic Cultism in Jamaica*, p. 63.

[15] *Ibid.*, p. 104.

[16] Leonard E. Barrett, *The Rastafarians: Sounds of Cultural Dissonance*, pp. 95 – 96.

[17] Leonard E. Barrett, *The Rastafarians: A Study in Messianic Cultism in Jamaica*, p. 138.

[18] Stephen Davis and Peter Simon, *Reggae Bloodlines*, pp. 76 – 77.

8

Positive Vibration

Most people think of Rastafarians in terms of ganja, dreadlocks, and reggae. Certainly these are the most obvious characteristics of the Rastafarian way of life, or *I-tal* living; and yet to better understand this Judeo-Christian cult that has prepared itself to usher in the apocalypse, one must discover what lies beneath the surface.

LIFESTYLE

The Rastafarians fashion their lifestyle after the ancient Israelites in terms of dietary law and hygiene. They are primarily vegetarians, for whom it is forbidden to eat meat, poultry, pork, or shellfish. On occasion they are permitted to eat fish, but only those fish smaller than twelve inches in length, with scales. Rastafarians consider larger fish that feed on smaller fish symbolic of the men of Babylon who feed on the lives of other men. It is also forbidden to consume alcoholic or stimulating beverages such as coffee, tea, or soda. The following is a verse from a Rastafarian song, which sees rum as poison:

> There is no comparison between ganja and rum
> The former keeps you cool, the latter makes you glum
> Rum as we know is an agent of death
> With the using of Ganja you draw new breath.[1]

I-tal (or total) food is, primarily, fresh, natural, and

89

unprocessed food from the plants of the earth. Indigenous fruits and vegetables are used in the Rastafarian diet including plantains (like bananas), papayas, breadfruit, oranges, ginger nuts, cho-chos, and calalloo. The Rastafarians combine their foods with a great understanding of their chemical and mineral nutrients, and the I-tal diet is claimed to provide protection from cancer. In fact, medicine and treatment of illness are handled exclusively through the use of diet and herbs. The Rasta believes that eating animal flesh causes one's stomach to become a cemetery and forces one to dedicate one's life to Babylon, which is doomed.

Faithful adherence to the I-tal diet is essential in order to hasten the process of purification and disassociation from the world of Babylon. Once this spiritual and physical weaning has taken place, the Rasta becomes free to move within the world of Babylon without being a part of it.

The Rastafarians also forbid the use of birth control because they believe killing the seed of life is an abomination. They say, "All sperm that go into a woman taking oral contraceptives will be dead. Where the dead have been buried? In the woman. So she become a sexpool of corruption . . . and man become the sex maniac. That's what a society of intellectuals produces. Them na can't produce more than corruption."[2]

Rastafarian women are treated much the same way in the Rasta community as the women of ancient Israel were treated in theirs. Women are forbidden to show their legs or wear mens' garments (such as pants or shorts) and must never enter a Rastafarian temple without their heads covered. They are allowed to smoke ganja only in private and never in the company of men. Women are completely subordinate in this male-oriented organization, and while it is an issue that must certainly come as an affront to many liberated twentieth century Western women, it is the Rastafarian women who must challenge this oppression and reveal it as paradoxical to the rest of the Rastafarian beliefs.

GANJA

Ganja is the sacrament of the Rastafarian brotherhood. The brethren gather and smoke *spliffs* (large hand-rolled cigars) of the fragrant herb ganga, imported from India centuries ago by a small band of Indian slaves. In India, the word *ganja* means marijuana and is often referred to as *Kali*, a name for the Indian goddess of destruction. She represents the hedonistic, sensual, and materialistic nature of man, the illusion of which must be consumed before it is transformed. Smoking ganja is the means of transformation.

To the Rastafarians, the herb is "the key to new understanding of the self, the universe, and God . . . Man basically is God, but this insight can come to man only with the use of the herb. When you use the herb, you experience yourself as God. With the use of the herb, you can exist in this dismal state of reality that now exists in Jamaica. You cannot change man, but you can change yourself with the use of the herb. When you are God, you deal with or relate to people like a god. In this way, you let your light shine, and when each of us lets his light shine, we are creating a god-like culture, and this is the cosmic unity that we try to achieve in the Rastafarian community."[3]

Rastafarians sanctify their use of ganja as a holy herb directly from the Bible. In Genesis 1:11–12 said, "Let the earth bring forth grass, the herb yielding seed, and the fruit tree yielding fruit after his kind, whose seed is in itself, upon the earth; and it was so . . . And God saw that it was good."

The Rasta reasoning follows that, "The divine sanction of the herb in the *Bible* . . . makes outlaws of governments who would forbid and suppress its use. It is thought that Babylon is afraid ganja will lead people to see the truth that living Babylon-way is a rotten way, an unholy way to live."[4] If the Jamaican authorities regard the Rastafarians as outlaws, then the Rastafarians see the Jamaican police in the same light.

Use of ganja is a viable means of obtaining a sense of liberation (or escape) for the Jamaican blacks who are inextricably caught in the web of Babylon's imperialist oppression on the island. Rastafarians believe that Jamaican blacks have been brainwashed by the white overlords — agents of Babylon — to believe themselves inferior and have been conditioned to accept European values. Rastafarians believe that smoking ganja brings deep healing and essential revelation, which releases them from the negative self-image that has kept blacks spiritually, socially, and economically imprisoned. It also restores in them a true love for the black race. One Dread says of ganja, "It gives I (and I) good meditation; it is a door inside, and when it is open you see everything that is good."[5] In the Book of Revelations 22:2 it is revealed, "In the midst of the street . . . was there the tree of life . . . and the leaves of the tree were for the healing of the nations."

DREADLOCKS

Certainly one of the most distinguishing characteristics of the Rastafarians are their dreadlocks. Cultivating lionlike manes, the Rastas let their hair grow long and do nothing but wash it, letting it dry in its natural state, which eventually results in a mass of long, knotted ringlets. According to Rastafarian code, no comb or razor must touch their heads. Drawing from the ways of the ancient Israelites, they faithfully follow Levitical Law, as found in the Old Testament, Leviticus 19:27. "Ye shall not round the corners of your heads, neither shalt thou round the corners of thy beard," and in Numbers 6:5, " . . . there shall no razor come upon his head; until the days be fulfilled . . . he shall be holy, and shall let the locks of the hair of his head grow."

Dreadlocks are carefully protected from Babylon and are usually worn tucked under a handmade tam that bears the Rastafarian colors of red, green, and gold. Red stands for the blood that has been shed in the name of black freedom; green represents the color of life and of ganja, the holy herb; and gold reflects the wisdom of Jah and the precious fragment of Him that dwells in every soul.

LANGUAGE

Among the Rastafarians, language is regarded as a holy tool, the importance of which is much beyond the function of mere communication. The most frequently used expression is "I and I," which has given the language its nickname *Iyaric*. I and I reflects the basic Monophysite belief of the Ethiopian Orthodox Church that the divine nature of God and the human nature of Jesus Christ are one and the same. In essence, this means that God dwells within each and every human being. In this way, everyone is capable of being or realizing God by searching for Him within the wisdom and purity of his own soul. So, the first "I" refers to the divine, the second "I" refers to the man, and together, the resulting union of "I and I" is the only way Rastafarians can talk about themselves and the world around them. The use of "I and I" is a constant reminder of the presence of Jah.

This concept is not entirely new. The Hindus often greet one another or say farewell with the blessing "Namaste," which means: The divine in me greets the divine in you, and in that place, we are one. This manner of speech is akin to the beliefs of the Ethiopian Orthodox Church and Haile Selassie, himself. Haile Selassie did not deny the possibility of his divinity resulting from and connected with being chosen emperor; however, when presented with the claim that he was the Messiah, the emperor was offended. Fundamentally, his claim to divinity was not exclusive. He believed that the manifestation of God is available to anyone and everyone who is a true seeker.

The most ritualized form of Rastafarian worship is *Nyabingi* or Holy Grounation. The word Nyabingi comes from the East African reference to a religious and political cult that resisted colonialism in the nineteenth century. Nyabingi meetings usually take place on a weekly basis, during which the brethren gather and smoke ganja, make *reasoning* (conversation), and immerse themselves in the tribal drumming rhythms of their ancestors. It is from these ancestral rhythms that reggae music gets its deep, resounding bass beat.

Before the first spliff is smoked, a benediction is said, "Glory to the father and to the maker of creation. As it was in the beginning, is now and ever shall be world without end: Jah Rastafari."[6]

There is an annual Nyabingi convention, or Grounation, to which Rastas from all over the island travel. Lasting from several days to a week, this meeting provides an arena for discussion or reasoning of an enlightened nature on the condition of the world (Jamaica in particular). It also involves feasting, chanting, and dancing. Since Haile Selassie's visit to Jamaica in 1966, this annual festival has taken place on April 21, the anniversary of his arrival. The concept of this Grounation is to give Rastas the opportunity to become grounded and centered in the Rastafarian nation. Although it is not a nation with political boundaries, the Rastafarian nation exists within its own way of life.

WORD, SOUND, AND POWER

The Rastafarians understand the phenomenon of word, sound, and power. It is their belief that positive use of words creates positive energy, and this may be the basis for reggae music, which is used as a tool to uplift the world through positive musical vibration.

The name Ras Tafari has become a familiar word to many people in the Western world, not because of their knowledge of Haile Selassie, but because of reggae music. Reggae has a hypnotic, moving beat that can engage a crowd through a deep, primal source while uplifting them to an ethereal state of consciousness. The power of reggae music comes from the musicians' belief in Jah and their dedication to His Imperial Majesty. To these musicians, reggae is Jah's gift and Jah's voice.

Perhaps the most well known of the musical prophets is Bob Marley. He and the other original members of the internationally known group, the Wailers — Peter (McIn-) Tosh, Bunny Livingston, and Junior Braithwaite — followed the teachings of their mentor, Rastafarian elder Joe Higgs, and were the first to bring the name of His Imperial Majesty into their music. Although they began playing together in 1964, they did not receive international acclaim until 1972 with the release of their first album, *Catch a Fire*, which was a brutally frank indictment of slavery and colonialism. They continued to tour around the world, and they released a total of eight albums, all on the Island Records label. Beside *Exodus*, perhaps the most important album for the Rastafarian movement is *Survival*, which came after an assassination attempt on Bob Marley's life in 1976. *Survival* was reviewed as "Marley's most thematically unified and ideologically daring work . . . This is bold stuff about staying free in a world made of chains."[7]

Bob Marley has become the voice of the third wave of the Rastafarian movement and a musical-political ambassador of the Third World. Full of hauntingly ancient wisdom and painfully contemporary insight, Bob Marley's lyrics frequently speak of the worlds of Babylon and Zion, the hell of the former and the earthly perfection of the latter. He believed that the children of Zion would be awakened through positive musical vibration and learn to transcend the destruction of Babylon. Realizing the ineffectiveness of direct confrontation with Babylon, Bob Marley cleverly disguised his political anger over the injustices dealt the blacks at the hand of white imperialists in the chanted lyrics of his songs.

Most reggae songs express one or two basic thoughts, repeated over and over again to completely saturate the consciousness of the listener. Some of these thoughts bear messages

Bob Marley, Musical prophet

Peter Tosh, Reggae musician

like Peter Tosh's when he sings "No matter where you come from, if you are a black man, you are an African." Black Uhuru tells listeners that "Darkness still circles round the world." Bob Marley reminds his followers to "Get up, stand up. Stand up for your rights." Jimmy Cliff advises, "Treat the youths right instead of giving them a fight, or it will be dynamite." He also warns in one song, "Peace will not be achieved through violence, otherwise the next generation will want revenge."

Bob Marley said, "The truth isn't homegrown, it's a universal language. Jah gave man his life forever. In the end, all men will sing the same song. In my music I want people to recognize themselves."[8] In a personal interview, Bob Marley said, "If God hadn't given me a song to sing, I wouldn't have a song to sing."[9] This Rasta musical prophet's animated and charismatic performance style has been described in the following manner: "The more one listens, the more one also realizes that his music and message come from beyond, from a totally spiritual inspiration. He moves onstage with the complete willingness to be a vehicle, to be carried back and forth across the stage in rhythmic, entrancing frenzy, as if governed by an inner light aimed at outwardly spreading the Rasta message."[10]

The reggae concert is like a ritualized Rastafarian mass during which the musicians serve as high priests. Usually before the concert begins, a benediction to Jah Rastafari is given, followed by a moment of silence. The audience is then swept away by an onslaught of reggae rhythm that continues for hours. As the audience dances cares and tensions away, the musicians infuse them with the wisdom of Jah, which promises deliverance from Babylon into Jah's Kingdom of Zion. The symbolism of the lyrics is often lost in the frenzy of the crowd, the thickness of the Jamaican accent, and the unusual language of the Iyaric. However, those in the audience accustomed to these characteristic elements find the experience of word, sound, and power overwhelming. It is considered to be an intense experience of divine light.

Not all Rastafarians are happy with what Bob Marley represents. Many totally committed Rastafarians believe that living a pure, simple, and consistent Rastafarian life is the only way to be a true Rastafarian. These brethren believe that true Rastafarians do not promote their music through Babylon. There are reggae musicians such as Burning Spear and Toots Hibbert of Toots and the Maytals who spend less time touring and more time at home in Jamaica living the Rastafarian way of life.

And yet one cannot deny that the Rastafarian movement would not have gained its worldwide popularity had it not been for Bob Marley, who defends his position saying, "You have fe be careful of the song you sing. And if Babylon come fe exploit us, it just make Babylon fall faster. If we are true brothers, money is not a separation for us."[11] Bob Marley has undeniably brought Jah Rastafari into the hearts and minds of many brothers and sisters around the world, regardless of race, of color, or of religious and intellectual beliefs. "Marley walks a fine line between the worlds of Jamaica and Babylon, and his triumphs and dilemmas ultimately reflect those of reggae as a whole."[12]

It was a great loss to the world of reggae, and a loss to the world at large, when Bob Marley died of brain cancer in January 1981. Fundamental to Rasta *overstanding* (the lyaric term for understanding) is that the spirit lives on. Bob Marley has undoubtedly been immortalized by the word, sound, and power of his music, which will continue to play its part in keeping the spirit of Jah Rastafari very much alive.

[1] Tracy Nicholas, *Rastafari: A Way of Life*, p. 142.

[2] *Ibid.*, p. 65.

[3] Leonard E. Barrett, *The Rastafarians: Sounds of Cultural Dissonance*, p. 217.

[4] Tracy Nicholas, *Rastafari: A Way of Life*, p. 51.

[5] *Ibid.*, p. 130.

[6] Leonard E. Barrett, *The Rastafarians: Sounds of Cultural Dissonance*, p. 148.

[7] Chris Morris, "Marley and Survival: The Grateful Dread."

[8] *Santa Cruz Sentinel*, (November 30, 1979), p. 21.

[9] Stephen Davis and Peter Simon, *Reggae Bloodlines*, p. 43.

[10] Chris Cioe and John Sutton-Smith, "Bob Marley and the Roots of Reggae," *Musician*, p. 42.

[11] Stephen Davis and Peter Simon, *Reggae Bloodlines*, p. 43.

[12] Chris Cioe and John Sutton-Smith, "Bob Marley and the Roots of Reggae," *Musician*, p. 42.

9

Babylon

The Rastafarians view their movement as apocalyptic, with Ras Tafari as deliverer. Before discussing the legitimacy of such a claim — specifically whether or not Haile Selassie is or was the Messiah — it is necessary to examine the apocalyptic symbolism of the Rastafarian view of the world, simplistically expressed through the polarity of their explanations of Babylon and Zion.

In studying the Rastafarian concept of Babylon, it is important to remember that the Rastafarians accept no interpretations of the Bible except those that endorse their beliefs. They believe that through the translations of the Bible from Greek to Latin to English, many corruptions have occurred to suit the vision of the translators. To be properly *overstood*, the Bible must be *correctly* interpreted. "The Bible therefore is a book of symbols of contemporary significance to which only the Rastafarians have the key,"[1] and ganja provides insight into this inherent truth.

To fully understand what is meant by the Rastafarian reference to Babylon, it is necessary to, once again, look at the Bible. The actual city of Babylon — founded by Nimrod and originally built in approximately 2,230 B.C., in Ur at the junction of the Tigres and Euphrates River of Mesopotamia — is often mentioned in the Old Testament. It is referred to with wonder and admiration of its splendor and advanced civilization. Yet, it is just as often referred to as a city of doom, owing to the godless and indulgent lifestyle of its inhabitants.

In the New Testament, Babylon became the symbolic name

for heathen Rome, where Jews were enslaved and early Christians persecuted. Ancient Rome eventually destroyed itself through excess and perversion, as practiced by the likes of Nero and Caligula.

The Rastafarians' use of the word Babylon alludes to their view of the entire Western socioeconomic system, which is built on oppression, exploitation, and manipulation of the masses for the benefit of the few. The Rastafarians believe that the white population is destined to destroy itself with nuclear weapons and that, eventually, only the black population will survive on this planet. Marcus Garvey said:

> In the very near future, we shall see the most bloody conflict ever waged by man. Whether it is to be a war of the races or of the nations, no one can tell, but so long as this injustice continues, so long as the strong continue to oppress the weak . . . and keep the more unfortunate of humanity in serfdom, and to rob and exploit them, so long will the cause of war be fed with the fuel of revenge, of hatred and of discontent.[2]

Central to Babylon's power is the Roman Catholic Church and the pope. Rastafarians even accused the pope of initiating Mussolini's plans to invade Ethiopia in 1936, with the supposed intention of recapturing the lost Ark of the Covenant. To the Rastas, the pope is the high priest of Babylon and a symbol of white supremacy.

THE BOOK OF REVELATION

Revelation 18:2-3 describes an angel of light coming down from heaven, lighting up the earth with his power, and describing his vision of Babylon on Earth:

> Babylon the great is fallen and is become the habitation of devils, and the hold of every foul spirit, and a cage of every unclean and hateful bird. For all nations have drunk of the wine [blood] of her fornication [exploitations], and the kings of the earth have committed fornication with her, and the merchants of the earth are waxed rich through the abundance of her delicacies.

Whether this quote refers to the European Common Market or the Catholic Church, no one really knows. Readers of the book of Revelation have been trying to interpret this passage for 2,000 years.

In Revelation 18:4, the angel goes on to say,

> Come out of her [Babylon] my people, that ye be not partakers of her sins, and that ye receive not of her plagues.

To the Rastafarians, this justifies their retreat from the European influence of Jamaican society, and all its inherent ills.

The symbol of the beast, Gog Magog, in Revelation 13, represents the governments of the world. The beast has seven heads, which are said to represent different eras of history, and ten horns. Upon each head is written the name of blasphemy, and upon each horn is a crown. The beast is also described as having the feet of a bear (Russia) and having been given his power by the red dragon (China). Two of the four holy beasts that sit around the throne of God are the lion (Africa) and the eagle (United States). The symbolic struggle of all these beasts represents the ultimate Battle of Armageddon and the ensuing destruction of Babylon.

Such a dismal world view requires some light to bring it into balance. There is a way out of Babylon as intimated by the following, taken from Revelation 5:2-5. This passage holds great symbolic significance for the Rastafarians and is frequently quoted by them:

> And I saw a strong angel proclaiming with a loud voice, 'Who is worthy to open the book and break the seals thereof?' And no man in heaven, nor in earth, neither under the earth, was able to open the book [of life], neither to look thereon. And I wept much, because no man was found worthy to open and read the book, neither to look thereon. And one of the elders said unto me, 'Weep not: Behold, the Lion of the tribe of Judah, the root of David, hath prevailed to open the book, and to loose the seven seals thereof.' . . . And they sang a new song, saying, 'Thou art worthy to take the book and open the seals thereof: . . . and we shall reign on earth.'

Rastafarians interpret this to mean that Haile Selassie, the Lion of Judah — descended from David through King Solomon and the Queen of Sheba — is the appointed Messiah and deliverer from Babylon. The book of life is a metaphor for the world, although to some it refers to the human being. According to this line of thought, the seven seals could be interpreted to represent the seven *chakras* (energy centers of the human body), as explained by the ancient Vedic wisdom of the Hindus. Strangely enough, the name "Haile Selassie" translates as the power of the Trinity, a suitably Christian reference in this context. It is on the basis of this passage that Haile Selassie qualifies as the Rastafarians' Messiah.

For the Rastafarians, the symbol of the four horsemen of the apocalypse proves that the black race is destined to inherit the earth. When the first of the seven seals of the book of life is opened, the first to emerge is the white horse. The rider of the white horse is armed with a bow and a crown upon his head, representing the European monarchies who went out to conquer the lands of the earth and bring them under their dominion. This rider with the bow and arrow, like a princely carrion, epitomizes the flesh eaters who thrive on the blood of their victims. The red horse of the second seal represents the communist nations. The rider holds a sword and is bent on killing and taking peace from the earth. The rider of the black horse, released by the third seal, carries a pair of balances, the scales representing justice. Rastafarians interpret this to mean that the black population is the real savior of the present world and that the black nations of earth will bring the inevitable healing after the fall of the beast. And finally, the pale horse, representing the Asian nations, is ridden by Death, who will kill with hunger and starvation.

Revelation 17:14 states that the beast will eventually be overcome by the lamb, which symbolizes God's chosen deliverer, who, to the Rastafarians, is Haile Selassie (the power of the Trinity).

As do the Hindus, Rastafarians see the incarnations of God in succession. First, God came to the Hebrews in the person of Moses, and second as the prophet Elijah, who was taken up into heaven by a chariot of fire. Next he came as Jesus Christ, who promised he would come again. This time, and the last time, he has come as Ras Tafari. Their belief in eternal life is expressed this way: "Even if a Rastafarian pass [sic] away because of old age, he really is not dead. The atoms of his body pass back into the totality of things. These atoms are again utilized into the formation of other new-born babies and life continues as before."[3] Perhaps this is why the Rastafarians seem to be undaunted by the demise and death of Haile Selassie. To them, he was betrayed by Babylon and has risen to a higher place from where he directs the wisdom and energy of Jah.

All true Rastafarians eventually meet in Zion. Zion is an ancient Hebrew place where a fortress was built. David captured the fortress and later built his palace there. It is figuratively used to represent the city of God, a spiritual city inhabited by God-realized beings. Once again in Revelation 14:1:

> I looked and behold, a Lamb stood on Mt. Zion, and with him 144,000 having his Father's name written on their foreheads, and I heard a voice from heaven as the voice of many waters, and as the voice of a great thunder: and I heard the voice of harpers playing their harps, and they sang a new song before the throne and before the four beasts and the elders and no man could learn that song but the 144,000 who were redeemed from the earth.

Babylon and Zion are recurring metaphors throughout both the Old and New Testaments of the Bible, and most symbolically in the book of Revelation of Saint John of the Apocalypse. Preaching the vision of the Apocalypse and relying heavily on the book of Revelation of Saint John, the Rastafarians represent an apex to a symbolically holy triangle that uses the Old Testament of the Jewish faith and the New Testament of the Christian faith as its foundation. Those who are neither devout Rastafarians nor familiar with the symbols of the Apocalypse will have a difficult time making sense of such abstract allegations, which fit nowhere within the framework of logic and fact. But, however academic your approach, it is useful to have these insights in order to better appreciate the lyrics of reggae music and to understand why the Rastafarians have chosen the lifestyle they embrace.

MYTH OR MESSIAH

An issue that continues to puzzle modern-day historians and sociologists is the deification of Haile Selassie. In many ways his tyrannical and dictatorial government epitomized Babylon, with its imperial elite and a landed aristocracy that exploited the masses. How can oppressed blacks worship a man who allowed nearly a million people to starve to death?

It is difficult to answer this question or provide justification for his incongruous philosophies. Perhaps Haile Selassie aimed too high, strived too hard, suffered too much, and grew old too soon. Perhaps he was just a man who chose to take on a nearly impossible challenge of uplifting the lives of his people. His solution to the backward social problems of Ethiopia was to educate Ethiopians so that, in time, they could take responsibility for these problems themselves. He saw the process of modernization as a slow and gradual one. It is unfortunate, but, perhaps, predictable that those groomed for this transformation became the very same people who destroyed him. In the face of civil war, the extermination of the Falashas, and a relentless communist rule, Ethiopia suffers under a more oppressive regime today than ever before. The devastating famine that began in 1972 still continues well into the 1980s, and refugees from Ethiopia reflect on the days of Haile Selassie as a golden era.

Haile Selassie was a private man. With what is known about him, biographers will have a difficult choice in portraying him as either an enlightened leader or a self-interested autocrat, a martyr or a monster. In any case, whatever is written about Haile Selassie will be interpreted and judged through the reader's viewpoint. The truth about him has yet to be revealed in an absolute way.

The roots of Rastafari stretch back to the dawn of history, through one of the most glorious civilizations man has known. The movement they spawned thrives today as one of the most contemporary of our times. The message of Jah through reggae is what perpetuates the immortality of Ras Tafari, the man. Yet, the Rastafarian movement is, indeed, more than just music. Rastafari embodies all of the ancient Judeo-Christian disciplines of diet, fasting, prayer, worship, vigilance, devotion, temperance, and compassion. Mastery of these disciplines and understanding of how they guide one to lead a just and spiritual life is the purpose of Rastafarian movement.

An underlying belief in freedom for all races has motivated an awakening of political consciousness among blacks in the west. The movement has gone beyond a purely Jamaican context and is now disseminating its message throughout the world. It is believed that, in essence, we are all sons and daughters of Jah, irrespective of color or race and that Babylon can be conquered simply by the correction of its spiritual imbalance. This correction is the responsibility of each and every individual, in the realm of his or her own life. Ras Tafari continues to live through this message which provides the impetus for all followers to discover their God within.

[1]Leonard E. Barrett, *The Rastafarians: A Study in Messianic Cultism in Jamaica*, p. 147.
[2]Amy Jacques-Garvey, ed., *Philosophy and Opinions of Marcus Garvey*, p. 33.
[3]*Ibid.*, p. 133.

Appendix

THE ODES OF SOLOMON

Taken from the *Forgotten Books of Eden*, the following selection of seven of the forty-two *Odes of Solomon* represent some of the most enchanting and mysterious biblical literature yet to be discovered. No one really knows who wrote the odes, or when. All that is known for certain about these lyrics is that they were passed down from generation to generation until they finally came to light as part of a Syriac document, translated long ago from the original Greek.

Strangely enough, the odes are derived neither from the Old Testament nor the Gospels, but seem to have a source uniquely their own. Some believe that the odes were sung by the early Christians of the first century A.D., which is obvious from their apocalyptic content and references to the Virgin Birth. However, the fact that the odes are attributed to Solomon might suggest that much of the wisdom in these poetic songs came from Solomon, himself, and from the traditions of the ancient Israelites. It is altogether possible that the Queen of Sheba experienced her conversion while listening to the chants from which these odes originated.

The Rastafarians believe in the word power of *chanting down* evil. Used in such a way, the odes can be as contemporary in their wisdom as is reggae. Their allusions to God are remarkably interchangeable with the spirit of Jah Rastafari.

ODE 12

An exceptionally high level of spiritual thought:

He hath filled me with words of truth; that I may speak the same:

And like the flow of waters flows truth from my mouth, and my lips show forth His fruit

And He has caused His knowledge to abound in me, because the mouth of the Lord is the true Word, and the door of His light;

And the Most High hath given it to His words, which are the interpreters of His own beauty, and the repeaters of His praise, and the confessors of His counsel, and the heralds of His thought, and the chasteners of His servants.

For the swiftness of the Word is inexpressible, and like its expression is its swiftness and force;

And its course knows no limit. Never doth it fail, but it stands sure, and it knows not descent nor the way of it.

For as its work is, so is its end: for it is light and the dawning of thought:

And by it the worlds talk one to the other; and in the Word there were those that were silent;

And from it came love and concord; and they spake one to the other whatever was theirs; and they were penetrated by the Word;

And they knew Him who made them, because they were in concord; for the mouth of the Most High spake to them; and His explanation ran by means of it:

For the dwelling-place of the Word is man: and its truth is love.

Blessed are they who by means thereof have understood everything, and have known the Lord in His truth. Hallelujah.

ODE 13

A strange little ode . . .

Behold! the Lord is our mirror: open the eyes and see them in Him: and learn the manner of your face:

And tell forth praise to His spirit: and wipe off the filth from your face: and love His holiness, and clothe yourselves therewith: And be without stain at all times before Him. Hallelujah.

ODE 19

Fantastic and not in harmony with the other Odes. The reference to a painless Virgin Birth is notable.

A cup of milk was offered to me: and I drank it in the sweetness of the delight of the Lord.

The Son is the cup, and He who was milked is the Father:

And the Holy Spirit milked Him: because His breasts were full, and it was necessary for Him that His milk should be sufficiently released;

And the Holy Spirit opened His bosom and mingled the milk from the two breasts of the Father; and gave the mixture to the world without their knowing:

And they who receive in its fullness are the ones on the right hand.

The Spirit opened the womb of the Virgin and she received conception and brought forth; and the Virgin became a Mother with many mercies;

And she travailed and brought forth a Son, without incurring pain;

And because she was not sufficiently prepared, and she had not sought a midwife (for He brought her to bear) she brought forth, as if she were a man, of her own will;

And she brought Him forth openly, and acquired Him with great dignity,

And loved Him in His swaddling clothes and guarded Him kindly, and showed Him in Majesty. Hallelujah.

ODE 20

A mixture of ethics and mysticism; of the golden rule and the tree of life.

I am a priest of the Lord, and to Him I do priestly service; and to Him I offer the sacrifice of His thought.

LOS GATOS H.S. LIBRARY

For his thought is not like the thought of the world nor the thought of the flesh, nor like them that serve carnally.

The sacrifice of the Lord is righteousness, and purity of heart and lips.

Present your reins before Him blamelessly: and let not thy soul to soul.

Thou shalt not acquire a stranger by the price of thy silver, neither shalt thou seek to devour thy neighbor,

Neither shalt thou deprive him of the covering of his nakedness.

But put on the grace of the Lord without stint; and come into His paradise and make thee a garland from its tree,

And put it on thy head and be glad; and recline on His rest, and glory shall go before thee,

And thou shalt receive of His kindness and of His grace; and thou shalt be flourishing in truth in the praise of His holiness.

Praise and honour be to His name. Hallelujah.

ODE 23

The reference to the sealed document sent by God is one of the great mysteries of the collection:

Joy is of the saints! and who shall put it on, but they alone?

Grace is of the elect! and who shall receive it except those who trust in it from the beginning?

Love is of the elect? And who shall put it on except those who have possessed it from the beginning?

Walk ye in the knowledge of the Most High without grudging: to His exultation and to the perfection of His knowledge.

And His thought was like a letter; His will descended from on high, and it was sent like an arrow which is violently shot from the bow:

And many hands rushed to the letter to seize it and to take and read it:

And it escaped their fingers and they were affrighted at it and at the seal that was upon it.

Because it was not permitted to them to loose its seal: for the power that was over the seal was greater than they.

But those who saw it went after the letter that they might know where it would alight, and who should read it and who should hear it.

But a wheel received it and came over it:

And there was with it a sign of the Kingdom and of the Government:

And everything which tried to move the wheel it mowed and cut down:

And it gathered the multitude of adversaries, and bridged the rivers and crossed over and rooted up many forests and made a broad path.

The head went down to the feet, for down to the feet ran the wheel, and that which was a sign upon it.

The letter was one of command, for there were included in it all districts;

And there was seen at its head, the head which revealed even the Son of Truth from the Most High Father,

And he inherited and took possession of everything. And the thought of many was brought to nought.

And all the apostates hasted and fled away. And those who persecuted and were enraged became extinct.

And the letter was a great volume, which was wholly written by the finger of god:

And the name of the Father was on it, and the Son and of the Holy Spirit, to rule for ever and ever. Hallelujah.

ODE 42

The Odes of Solomon, the Son of David, are ended with the following exquisite verses.

I stretched out my hands and approached my Lord: for the stretching of my hands is His sign:

My expansion is the outspread tree which was set up on the way of the Righteous One.

And I became of no account to those who did not take hold of me; and I shall be with those who love me.

All my persecutors are dead; and they sought after me who hoped in me, because I was alive:

And I rose up and am with them; and I will speak by their mouths.

For they have despised those who persecuted them; and I lifted up over them the yoke of my love;

Like the arm of the bridegroom over the bride,

So was my yoke over those that know me:

And as the couch that is spread in the house of the bridegroom and bride,

So is my love over those that believe in me.

And I was not rejected though I was reckoned to be so.

I did not perish, though they devised it against me.

Sheol saw me and was made miserable;

Death cast me up and many along with me.

I had gall and bitterness, and I went down with him to the utmost of his depth:

And the feet and the head he let go, for they were not able to endure my face:

And I made a congregation of living men amongst his dead men, and I spake with them by living lips:

Because my word shall not be void:

And those who had died ran towards me: and they cried and said, Son of God, have pity on us, and do with us according to thy kindness,

And bring us out from the bonds of darkness: and open to us the door by which we shall come out to thee.

For we see that our death has not touched thee.

Let us also be redeemed with thee: for thou art our Redeemer.

And I heard their voice; and my name I sealed upon their heads:

For they are free men and they are mine. Hallelujah.

ODE 6

First century universalism is revealed in an interesting way.

As the hand moves over the harp, and the strings speak, So speaks in my members the Spirit of the Lord, and I speak by His love.

For it destroys what is foreign, and everything that is bitter:

For thus it was from the beginning and will be to the end, that nothing should be His adversary, and nothing should stand up against Him.

The Lord has multiplied the knowledge of Himself, and is zealous that these things should be known, which by His grace have been given to us.

And the praise of His name He gave us: our spirits praise His holy spirit.

For there went forth a stream and became a river great and broad;

For it flooded and broke up everything and it brought [water] to the Temple:

And the restrainers of the children of men were not able to restrain it, nor the arts of those whose business it is to restrain waters;

For it spread over the face of the whole earth, and filled everything; and all the thirsty upon earth were given drink of it;

And thirst was relieved and quenched; for from the Most High the draught was given.

Blessed then are the ministers of that draught who are entrusted with that water of His:

They have assuaged the dry lips, and the will that had fainted they have raised up;

And souls that were near departing they have caught back from death:

And limbs that had fallen they straightened and set up:

They gave strength for their feebleness and light to their eyes:

For everyone knew them in the Lord, and they lived by the water of life for ever. Hallelu-JAH.

Bibliography

1. Asante, S. K. B. *Pan-African Protest: West Africa and the Italo-Ethiopian Crises, 1934–1941.* London: Longman Group Ltd., 1977.

2. Barker, A. J. *The Civilizing Mission.* New York: Dial Press, 1968.

3. Barrett, Leonard E. *The Rastafarians: A Study in Messianic Cultism in Jamaica.* Rio Piedras, Puerto Rico: University of Puerto Rico, 1963.

4. Barrett, Leonard E. *The Rastafarians: Sounds of Cultural Dissonance.* Boston: Beacon Press, 1977.

5. Bergsma, Stuart. *Rainbow Empire.* Grand Rapids, Michigan: William B. Erdmans Publishing Co., 1932.

6. Budge, Sir E.A. Wallis. *History of Ethiopia.* 2 vols. Oosterhout, The Netherlands: Anthropological Publications, 1966.

7. Buxton, David. *The Abyssinians.* New York: Praeger Publishers, 1970.

8. Cioe, Chris and Sutton-Smith, John. "Bob Marley and the Roots of Reggae." *Musician.* pp. 42–46.

9. Constitutional Developments in Ethiopia. *Africa Research Bulletin*, Sept. 1–30, 1974.

10. Davis, Stephen and Simon, Peter. *Reggae Bloodlines*. Garden City, New York: Anchor/Doubleday, 1977.

11. Dugan, James. *Days of Emperor and Clown*. Garden City, New Jersey: Doubleday, 1973.

12. "Focus on Ethiopia: End of Feudal Era." *Bulletin of the African Institute*, November 7, 1975.

13. Hansberry, William Lee. *Pillars in Ethiopian History*. Washington D.C.: Howard University Press, 1974.

14. Hess, Robert L. *Ethiopia*. Ithica, New York: Cornell University Press, 1970.

15. Jacques-Garvey, Amy, ed. *Philosophy and Opinions of Marcus Garvey*. New York: Atheneum Books, 1969.

16. Kaplan, Irving, ed. *Ethiopia: A Country Study*. Washington D.C.: American University, 1981.

17. Mosley, Leonard O. *The Conquering Lion*. Englewood Cliffs, New Jersey: Prentice Hall, 1964.

18. Nicholas, Tracy. *Rastafari: A Wca Institute*, (November 7, 1975), pp. 243-244.

19. Schwab, Peter. *Haile Selassie*. Chicago: Nelson-Hall, 1979.

20. Shepherd, Jack. *The Politics of Starvation*. Washington D.C.: Carnegie Endowment for International Peace, 1975.

21. Ullendorf, Edward. *The Ethiopians*. London: Oxford University Press, 1960.

22. White, Timothy. "Bob Marley (1945-1981): The King of Reggae Finds His Zion." *Rolling Stone*, No. 346 (June 25, 1981), pp. 25–27.

Glossary

A

Abba Salama — literally, "Revealer of the Light"; the holy name given to the foreigner, Frumentius, who landed, shipwrecked, in Ethiopia in the fourth century A.D. Abba Salama went on to convert King Ezana to Christianity in 333 A.D.

Abuna — the title given to the archbishop of the Ethiopian Orthodox Church. The first abuna was Abba Salama. It was not unitl 1950, that Haile Selassie gained the power to select the abuna from within Ethiopia, independent of the sanction of the Egyptian Coptic Church of Alexandria.

Abyssinia — the ancient classical name for Ethiopia; more commonly used by foreigners (Europeans) than by natives, who prefer to call themselves Ethiopians. To an Ethiopian, to be called an Abyssinian is an insult.

Addis Ababa — literally, "New Flower"; the capital of Ethiopia, located in the central Ethiopian highlands in the province of Shoa. Menelik II established Addis Ababa as the capital at the turn of the century.

Adowa — site of the brutal and humiliating defeat in 1896 of the Italians by the Ethiopians under the leadership of Ras Makonnen and Menelik II located in the provence of Gojjam near the Eritrean border.

Amharic — the official popular language of Ethiopia and the primary language of the aristocratic Shoans; used both conversationally and in the written press. Countless other local dialects are used among tribes in the different provinces of Ethiopia.

Angabo — the legendary hero who slew the evil serpent Wainaba and established his family as the Ethiopian royal line; ancestor of the infamous Queen of Sheba, whose son officially began the Ethiopian dynasty that lasted 3,000 years, through the reign of Haile Selassie.

Aphilas — the great-grandfather of King Ezana; lived at the end of the third century A.D.; famous for extending the Ethiopian empire across the Red Sea into Yemen on the South Arabian peninsula.

Asfa Wossen — the crown prince, Haile Selassie's eldest son. Because of Asfa's participation in a conspiracy to overthrow the emperor in 1960, Haile Selassie was reluctant to pass the throne on to him. Asfa Wossen never ruled as emperor, due to the rise of the PMAC.

Axum — also spelled Aksum; the ancient capital of Ethiopia, established by the Queen of Sheba's son, Menelik I. Site of ancient ruins, of obelisklike pillars called "stele," and of ancient libraries filled with rare religious manuscripts that were mostly destroyed by Moslems in the sixteenth century. The lost Ark of the Covenant is rumored to be buried somewhere in Axum.

B

Babylon — the Rastafarians' metaphysical reference for hell; all that is materialistic, self-serving, and decadent in modern Western society; doomed to destruction because of its exploitative nature. In the Old Testament, the city of Babylon was doomed because of its people's godless attitudes.

Badoglio — the Italian general who led the invasion of Ethiopia in

1936 and headed the Italian occupation until 1941. Starvation and adverse weather conditions eventually weakened the Italian troops sufficiently to allow Haile Selassie to return from exile and reassume the throne in 1941.

Belkis — the South Arabian name for the Queen of Sheba; described in less flattering terms than in Ethiopian legend.

C

Council of Ministers — the ruling governmental body in Ethiopia; comprised of the local aristocratic Shoan chiefs and powerful enough to depose and reappoint emperors; replaced by the Derg in 1974, after the downfall of Haile Selassie.

Cush — the Egyptian name for the "land of those with burnt faces"; Cushites are thought of as black. Biblically, Cush was one of the sons of Ham, (son of Noah), who established a kingdom between the second and fourth cataracts of the nile, after the Great Flood. The name "Ethiopia" is derived from Ethiops, Cush's son.

D

Derg — the governing body that deposed Haile Selassie in 1974; controlled by the PMAC, and oriented to a Marxist/Leninist philosophy.

Djibouti — one of the main ports for Ethiopia on the Gulf of Aden; located in French Somaliland.

Dreadlocks — the hair of Rastafarian men. A source of pride and distinction, proper dreadlocks are neither combed nor cut, and fall in a mass of long ringlets; their length signifies the extent of a man's holiness, causing "dread" in the unholy. In the everyday world of Babylon, dreadlocks are tucked inside a protective tam, usually made of the Rastafarian colors — red, green, and gold.

E

Ebna Hakim — literally, "Son of the Wise Man"; the birth-name of Menelik I, son of King Solomon and the Queen of Sheba.

Eritrea – a vital yet rebellious province along the Red Sea that continually seek independence from Ethiopia. Coastal access to the Red Sea makes Eritrea's ports of Massawa and Assab vital to Ethiopia.

Ethiops – one of the sons of Cush, who allegedly established a kingdom at the Nile's headwaters. Ethiopia derives its name from Ethiops. Aksumawi, the son of Ethiops, established the ancient city of Axum (Aksum).

Ezana – ruler of Ethiopia in the fourth century; responsible for Ethiopia's conversion to Christianity. In response to the teachings of Abba Salama, King Ezana declared Christianity the state religion in 333 A.D., around the time Constantine converted the Roman Empire to Christianity.

F

Falashas – the "black Jews" of Ethiopia; an ancient Semitic cult that lives in the Lake Tana region at the headwaters of the Nile and observes strict orthodox Hebrew practices. They may be descendants of Noah or one of the lost "ten tribes of Israel." Persecution by Ethiopia's current government threatens their existence.

Fasilidas – the son of King Susenyos, who massacred 8,000 of his own people for refusing to convert from the Ethiopian Orthodox Church of Roman Catholicism in the seventeenth century (due to pressure from the Portuguese.) When Fasilidas pointed out this hypocrisy to Susenyos, he renounced Catholicism and abdicated the throne to his son.

Ferengi – Amharic for "foreigner"; an insult reflecting the Ethiopians' inherent distrust of foreigners, such as Italians and Portuguese.

Frumentius – Abba Salama before his ordination as the first Abuna in the fourth century A.D. Frumentius arrived, shipwrecked, in Ethiopia with his brother, Edesius, and his uncle, Meropius.

G

Gallas – a native tribe inhabiting the interior of Ethiopia, including the provinces of Gojjam, Shoa, Harar, and Sidamo. Considered somewhat savage, the Gallas allegedly emasculated wounded Italian soldiers at the Battle of Adowa in 1896.

Ganja – the sacred herb of the Rastafarians; also known as marijuana. Ganja, dreadlocks, and reggae distinguish the Rastafarian lifestyle. Since smoking ganja is seen as a biblically sanctified sacrament, the Rastafarians are trying to obtain legal exemptions from traditional laws for its possession, cultivation, and use.

Garvey, Marcus – a radical Jamaican thinker who laid the foundations for the Rastafarian movement through his prophecy, "Look to Africa, when a black king is crowned, for the day of deliverance is near." This prophecy was made in 1929, the year before Haile Selassie's coronation.

Ge'ez – the ancient liturgical language of Ethiopia, somewhat like Latin. Gnostic monks translated many ancient religious manuscripts into Ge'ez.

Girmame Neway – conspired with his brother to overthrow Haile Selassie in December 1960, while the emperor was on a state visit to Brazil. Many high officials were implicated in the plot, including the Emperor's own son, Asfa Wossen.

Gnostic – a mystical religious sect of Christianity, whose monks sought direct experience of God through private worship, intense fasting, and meditation. Persecution in Europe over the principle of Monophysitism forced the Gnostics to flee to Ethiopia where they took refuge in the rock-hewn churches made by Lalibela, and there translated a great number of religious books into Ge'ez. Gnosis means "knowledge" in Greek.

Gojjam – one of the largest provinces in Ethiopia, located in the northwest interior on the highland plateau, bordering modern-day Sudan; originally populated by the Habasha of South Arabia.

Grounation – the affirmation of life through the earth; takes place

place annually on April 21 when the Rastas gather in the countryside to commemorate Haile Selassie's visit to Jamaica in 1966.

Ras Gugsa — son-in-law to Haile Selassie. When the Italians invaded Ethiopia in 1936, he provided them with vital maps and destroyed communication lines. Jealousy and resentment toward the emperor thought to be the motive. Some resentment stems from the emperor's treatment of Gugsa's first wife, Zauditu, when the emperor was Regent Ras Tafari. See *Zauditu*.

H

Habasha — the Semitic tribe from South Arabia that first migrated into the Ethiopian region of Gojjam; one of the earliest tribes to populate the highland plateau. The Habasha passed on to the Ethiopians the Himyaritic alphabet and their fine facial features.

Haile Selassie — literally, "Power of the Trinity;" the throne name chosen by Ras Tafari.

Harar — the Ethiopian province where Ras Tafari was born, and where his father, Ras Makonnen, ruled as governor. During the reign of his cousin, Lij Yasu, Ras Tafari became governor of Harar and there his first son was born.

Howell, Leonard — the leader of the early Rastafarian movement in Kingston, Jamaica. In the 1930s after studying the Bible, Howell decided that Ras Tafari was a genuine Messiah. Along with Archibald Dunkley, Joseph Hibbert, and Robert Hinds, he took to the streets preaching Rastafari. In 1940 Howell started the Pinnacle community, conceived of as a commune that existed outside the laws of Babylon.

I

I-tal — a colloquial Rasta term meaning "kosher" or in harmony with the Rastafarian way of life; derived from the word "total," or "natural," but prefixed with "I." the use of "I" refers to the Monophysite concept that "I" the human and "I" the divine are one. Hence the Rastas talk about themselves as "I and I," signifying a union with Jah.

Iyaric — the term for "Rasta talk." Its Principal use is in the frequent reference to "I and I" and I-tal food, but it also embraces other Rasta concepts such as "reasoning" (enlightened conversation), "overstanding" (as opposed to understanding), "to go forward" (instead of to go back), and "seen' (which means, "I know," in the way the French say "D'accord").

J

Jah — the Rastafarian name for God, probably derived from the ancient Hebrew name for God, Jah-weh; a guiding, omnipresent intelligence. Jah Ras Tafari means Ras Tafari, the Messiah, or Ras Tafari as God, or the god within Ras Tafari. Common is the belief that "Jah provides."

Jihad — the Moslem word for "holy war," a war executed to please or do the will of God. Jihad is destructive, brutal, and savage, as the Ethiopians experienced in the destruction of ancient Axum by Gran the Left-Handed in the sixteenth century.

K

Kebra Nagast — literally, "Glory of the Kings"; the most famous legend from the Ethipian Royal Chronicles; the book depicting the love story of King Solomon and the Queen of Sheba, and telling of their son, who became Menelik I, the first emperor of Ethiopia 3,000 years ago.

L

Lalibela — the architect of the magnificent rock-hewn churches in the region of Lasta that were carved out of living rock and considered to be one of the Seven Wonders of the Ancient World. Lalibela was one of the last kings of the Agau dynasty. There is a town named after him in Ethiopia.

Lij Yasu — grandson and successor of Emperor Menlik II upon his death in 1912. Despite power struggles with the emperor's widow, Taitu, and the young Ras Rafari, Yasu retained control until 1916 when he attempted to convert Ethiopia to Islam. Deposed by the Council of Ministers who appointed Ras Tafari as ruling regent, Yasu's downfall was due promptly to his decadent lifestyle and flagrant disregard for the ethics of leadership.

M

Magdala — site of Ras Makonnen's siege of the Italians in the late nineteenth century; located in the province of Lasta, near Dessye.

Ras Makonnen — Ras Tafari's father; nephew to Emperor Menelik II; defeated the Italians both at Adowa and Magdala. Ras Makonnen died suddenly and mysteriously in 1903 when Tafari was only fourteen years old.

Bob Marley — the legendary musical phophet of reggae; died of cancer in 1982. During the 1970s, with his group, the Wailers, Bob Marley popularized the message of the Rastafarians by bringing the Word-Sound-Power of Jah to a level of international awareness.

Massawa — a vital Ethiopian trading port on the coast of the Red Sea in the province of Eritrea.

Menelik I — Ethiopia's first emperor; founder of the Solomonic line of Ethiopian royalty. Born as Ebna Hakim, his parents were King Solomon and the Queen of Sheba.

Menelik II — the emperor who preceded Haile Selassie; a fierce warrior and strong leader who brought greater unity to Ethiopia's fourteen provinces than had existed for centuries; died in 1912.

Menen — the woman to whom Haile Selassie was devoted; during fifty years of marriage, she bore him five children.

Mengistu Haile Miriam — the leader of the PMAC after Haile Selassie was deposed in 1974; still the man in power in present-day Ethiopia.

Mengistu Neway — with his brother, instigated the rebellion against Haile Selassie in 1960, implicated the crown prince. When the attempted coup failed, his brother Girmame was shot and killed while trying to escape and Mengistu was later tried and executed. Ironically, Mengistu had been a trusted member of His Majesty's Imperial Body Guard for fifteen years.

Meroe — the island kingdom located between the fifth and sixth cataracts of the Nile, just downstream from the modern-day Khartoum in the Sudan. In ancient times, Meroe was a powerful kingdom ruled by a line of women known as the Candace queens. This black civilization was controlled by the Amen priesthood, which became corrupt and dictatorial, leading to Meroe's decline in the fourth century A.D.

Ras Mikael — the father of Lij Yasu, otherwise known as the "arrogant prince"; gained political power by making his son emperor from 1911-1916.

Monophysitism — the belief that each human being possesses a fragment of the divine within; God is manifest through Jesus Christ, but any human being can still discover God within. (In contrast, Roman Catholics believe that a human being can only discover God through Jesus and that left alone he or she is a hopeless sinner.) A schism in the Christian church brought about by these conflicting beliefs occured at the Councils of Nicea Chalcedon in the fourth century A.D. The Monophysites separated from the Roman Catholics and Byzantines to form the Coptic Church, centered in Alexandria, Egypt. The Ethiopian Orthodox Church drew its traditions from the Coptic Church.

Mussolini — the Italian dictator who initiated the invasion and occupation of Ethiopia in 1936 to further his own political ambitions; became an ally of Germany's Adolf Hitler, forming the Axis power in World War II.

N

Napata — the trading capital of Cush, located at the fourth cataract of the Nile River.

Negusa Nagast — literally, "the King of the Kings," loosely translated, "emperor." When Ethiopia was a collection of fourteen provinces, each had its own king, and the negusa nagast was the king of all fourteen kings. The negusa nagast was usually crowned on an ancient stone throne in Axum.

Neway — was the surname of the brothers, Girmame and Mengistu, who conspired to overthrow Haile Selassie in 1960. See both *Girmame* and *Mengistu.*

Nine Saints — the Gnostic monks who fled to Ethiopia from persecution in Europe during the Middle Ages; Abba Aleph, Abba Sehma, Abba Aragawi, Abba Afse, Abba Garima, Abba Pantalewon, Abba Likanos, Abba Guba, and Abba Yemata. They took refuge in the rock-hewn churches and monasteries built by Lalibela in the region of Lasta.

Nu — an Egyptian term referring to "the mothers and fathers of the great beyond, beyond the fringes of the known world," probably the land of Cush or Nubia located further upstream along the Nile. The ancestors could be the sons of Noah, Ham, Cush, and Mizraim. According to legend, the sons of Noah settled at the headwaters of the Nile, a place the Egyptians regarded as the source of all life, after the Great Flood.

Nubia — literally, "the land of gold." Lower Nubia was located in Egypt between the first and second cataracts of the Nile; Upper Nubia between the second and fourth cataracts, well within the land of Cush.

Nyabingi — the essential rhythm of life, emanating from the earth to the sky; the Rastafarian worship ritual of drumming, dancing, meditation, and chanting; usually beginning with a benediction and smoking spliffs of ganja, which will elicit "reasoning" (enlightened conversation), throughout the worship ritual.

O

Ogaden — one of the fourteen provinces of Ethiopia, located in the southeast bordering Somaliland; the source of an ongoing border dispute between Ethiopia and Somalia.

P

PMAC — the Provisional Military Administrative Council which controls the Derg; responsible for initiating the overthrow of Haile Selassie's regime in 1974. The PMAC's leader is Mengistu Haile Miriam, who made an alliance with the Soviet Union in 1977.

Q

Queen of Sheba — literally "south"; known as "Queen of the South"; name could have been derived from the coastal town of Assab. The matriarch who established the Solomonic line of the Ethiopian royal family through the birth of Ebna Hakim, who, as Menelik I, became Ethiopia's first emperor. Her relationship with King Solomon of Israel is one of the classic love stories of all time.

R

Ras — means "lord" or "sir"; a distinction of aristocracy, usually reserved for the Shoan class of Ethiopia, and accompanied by political and social power. Among the Rastafarians, ras usually means "spiritual brother"; it does not refer to political or social power, but rather to spiritual power.

Rastafari — the worshipers of Jah Ras Tarfari as the chosen Messiah referred to in the Book of Revelation in the New Testament. Rastafarians refer to themselves as the Rastafari.

S

Shankalla — the lower or slave class in Ethiopia; usually negroid; looked down upon by the upper classes.

Shoa — location of the Ethiopian capital, Addis Ababa; the province in the heart of Ethiopia, on the highland plateau. Home of the Shoan aristocracy who traditionally controlled the government and comprised the Council of Ministers, Ethiopia's ruling governmental body that appointed Ras Tafari as regent and later emperor.

Sidamo — the Ethiopian province ruled by Ras Tafari at the age of fourteen; located in the southwestern corner of Ethiopia, along the border of Kenya. He was given the governorship of this province by Menelik II, who wanted to protect him from the vicious power struggle taking place in Addis Ababa.

Spliff — the Rasta term for "joint" or "reefer"; giant-size joints usually rolled of fresh, homegrown ganja or "herb." See *ganja.*

Stele — the mysterious obelisklike pillars strewn among the ancient ruins of Axum; may have been altars or shrines. Many had the pagan symbol of the crescent moon cradling a sun-shaped disc engraved at the top.

Susenyos — the Ethiopian king converted to Roman Catholicism by the Portuguese in the 17th century. In his zeal to persuade fellow Ethiopians to abandon the Ethiopian Orthodox Church and embrace Catholicism, Susenyos massacred 8,000 of his own people. When he realized the hypocrisy of his own holy war, he abdicated the throne to his son, Fasilidas. See *Fasilidas.*

T

Tafari — the name given to Haile Selassie at birth. As a child, he took his father's first name as his surname (a common practice in Ethiopia), becoming Tafari Makonnen. When Tafari was appointed governor of Harar at age eighteen, he was given the title, ras, and then became known as Ras Tafari. See *ras.*

Taitu — the wife of Emperor Menelik II. As her husband's health deteriorated, Queen Taitu aspired to gain control of the royal court in Addis Ababa. She had her daughter, Zauditu, installed as Empress after Lij Yasu was thrown out of power in 1916.

Takla Haymanot — the powerful abuna who allegedly restored the Solomonic dynasty to the throne in the thirteenth century A.D., in exchange for one-third of the kingdom (which became church lands, exempt from taxation). Although the coup was bloodless, one can only wonder how the Agau ruler, Nekueto Laab, abdicated to the new Zagwé king, Yekuno Amlak.

Tamrin – a merchant and chief advisor to the Queen of Sheba; who first told to Queen about the amazing King Solomon, who worshipped the one true God of the Hebrews, Jehovah. Sheba then traveled to Israel to discover Solomon for herself.

Tanana – the sister of Emperor Menelik II; mother of Ras Makonnen; aunt of Tafari; through Tanana, Ras Tafari claims his royal ancestry.

Tej – a popular local alcoholic drink; a fermented wine that tastes like cider; apparently very potent.

Tigre – one of the oldest provinces in Ethiopia, located in the northeast next to Eritrea; site of the ancient city of Axum. In Tigre, the local dialect if Tigrinya is spoken.

U

UNIA – the Universal Negro Improvement Association. Founded in the United States by Marcus Garvey, UNIA flourisheed in the 1920s, growing to a membership of one million. Its philosophy was repatriation; its slogan was "Back to Africa!" Garvey organized the Black Star Line to transport UNIA members to a colony in Liberia, but treachery aborted Garvey's plans, and discredited him and the UNIA. Imprisoned on charges of fraud, Garvey was pardoned by President Calvin Coolidge in return for the UNIA's political support during his election.

W

Wainaba – the evil serpent monster slain by Angabo, who then became King. Angabo was the ancestor of the Queen of Sheba.

Y

Yemen – the region of the southern Arabian peninsula across the Red Sea; the early inhabitants – Habasha – of Ethiopia's highland plateau migrated from Yemen, bringing with them the Himyaritic alphabet and the fine Semitic features characteristic of the Ethipian people. Some of the lost Ten Tribes of Israel may have strayed to Yemen.

Z

Zauditu — translates as "Judith"; Queen Taitu's daughter; became empress in 1916 after Lij Yasu was deposed. With Ras Tafari as her Regent, she remained in power (as the political puppet of her mother) until she died in 1930. Her death was suspicious, and many suspected Ras Tafari; although she allegedly died as a result of a Lenten fast she would not end. Zauditu had been forbidden to see her husband, Ras Gugsa, who had been lured out of the palace by Ras Tafari to participate in a drunken orgy.

Zion — the metaphysical heaven of the Rastafarians. In opposition to Babylon, Zion is a utopian state of existence reflected by peace, brotherhood, unity, and enlightenment. Zion will be created on earth after the fall of Babylon. A similar reference in the Bible (in the Book of Revelation), is Mt. Zion, the place of redemption for the 144,000 who survive the Apocalypse.

LOS GATOS H.S. LIBRARY

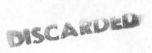